New research on Cornish architecture
Celebrating Pevsner

New research on Cornish architecture
Celebrating Pevsner

Papers from the 2015 Cornish Buildings Group conference 'Only a Cornishman would have the endurance to carve intractable granite'

Edited by Paul Holden

Francis Boutle Publishers

First published by Francis Boutle Publishers
272 Alexandra Park Road
London N22 7BG
Tel/Fax: (020) 8889 7744
Email: info@francisboutle.co.uk
www.francisboutle.co.uk

Copyright © Contributors, 2017

All rights reserved.
No part of this book may be reproduced, stored
in a retrieval system, or transmitted, in any form
or by any means, electronic, mechanical
photocopying or otherwise without the prior permission of the publishers.

ISBN 978 0 9957473 2 6

Acknowledgements

This volume has its origins in a two day conference organised in March 2015 by the Cornish Buildings Group. Its purpose was to celebrate the publication of Peter Beacham's 2014 revision of Nikolaus Pevsner's *Buildings of England, Cornwall*, first published in 1951. We are grateful to the Cornwall Heritage Trust, Yale University Press and the National Trust for supporting the conference. The event was hosted by the National Maritime Museum, Falmouth.

We would particularly like to thank all speakers for their enthusiastic lectures and scholarly contributions to this volume. Much of the positive feedback we received on the day related to the chronology and relevance of the conference papers, a formula that we have replicated in these proceedings. We would also like to thank the capacity audience who embraced the speakers and their subjects, extending the conference threads with learned questions and debate.

We would like to thank our publisher, Clive Boutle of Francis Boutle Publishers, for taking this project forward, thereby disseminating the conference papers to a much wider audience. Thanks to Sue Lightfoot for undertaking the indexing.

This volume is dedicated to Veronica Chesher who has done an enormous amount to further the study of Cornish architectural history.

Contents

3 Foreword – *John Stengelhofen*
5 Sources
7 List of illustrations
11 Introduction – *Paul Holden*
17 A Brief History of the Pevsner Architectural Guides – *Charles O'Brien*
23 A Personal Reflection on Revising *Cornwall* – *Peter Beacham*
31 'A large block of granite' or a unique piece of sculpture? – *Ann Preston-Jones*
41 Beasts and Beakheads: Romanesque Sculpture at Morwenstow – *Alex Woodcock*
49 Exeter Cathedral and church architecture in Cornwall in the early 14th century – *John Allan*
65 'The Longest, Strongest and Fairest that the Shire Could Muster – Wade-Bridge' – *Andrew Langdon*
74 If only Pevsner had started in the Midlands: making sense of Cornwall's perpendicular church architecture – *Joanna Mattingly*
83 'Ghastly Good Taste': the Cornish country house 1540–1840 – *Paul Holden*
93 Gothic Survival or Revival in Cornwall? – *Patrick Newberry*
103 A Victorian Vision Re-discovered: the stained glass windows of St Carantoc, Cornwall – *Michael G. Swift*
112 George Wightwick (1802–72) 'an architect of much ability and a man of exquisite taste' – *Rosamund Reid*
121 A Cornish Connoisseur and Builder: Lieutenant-Colonel Charles Lygon Cocks (1821–85) – *Jeremy Pearson*
130 Goth or Vandal? A re-appraisal of James Piers St Aubyn and Cornwall's Anglican churches. – *Michael Warner.*
137 East Cornwall Churches: does lightning strike twice? – *Simon Crosbie*
146 Biographies of contributors
149 Index

Foreword

John Stengelhofen

In the introduction to the new *Cornwall*, Peter Beacham notes 'The Cornish Buildings Group has a proud record of encouraging good design as well as opposing the destruction of the historic environment, no easy task in a county that was slow to appreciate its architectural and buildings heritage…'.[1] As we head towards our fiftieth year we are indeed 'proud' of our achievements. Our annual awards scheme has become a nationally recognised showcase for good design, our casework has become renowned by local authority, statutory consultees and pressure groups alike and our support and recognition has grown as a result.

Our conference was, in part, a consequence of this success and a long overdue celebration of our architectural heritage. The essays presented here, all written by experts in their respective fields, capture perfectly what we cherish most about Cornwall's sense of place and its built environment. It is however, an environment that is severely under threat from an archaic and under-resourced planning system. I hope that with the publication of these papers we can move forward with an informed view of the past.

The popularity of our conference is a testament to the high esteem that the *Buildings of England* series and the Cornish Buildings Group are held within the county. As former Chairman I would like to thank Paul Holden for his rigorous efforts in organising the conference and for his exacting standards in editing this volume.

1. Pevsner (2014), p,85.

Sources

Some books and sources appear regularly across all papers so are abbreviated as follows:

CRO – Cornwall Record Office.
Harries, Pevsner (2011) – Susie Harries, *Nikolaus Pevsner: The Life*, (London, 2011)
NA – National Archives, Kew, London.
Pevsner (1951) – Nikolaus Pevsner, *The Buildings of England: Cornwall* (Harmondsworth, 1951)
Pevsner (1970) – Nikolaus Pevsner revised by Enid Radcliffe, *The Buildings of England: Cornwall* (Harmondsworth, 1970).
Pevsner (2014) – Peter Beacham and Nikolaus Pevsner, *The Buildings of England: Cornwall* (New Haven and London, 2014).

Porth-en-Alls by Philip Tilden. A remarkable piece of 20th-century design overlooking Prussia Cove. John Stengelhofen.

List of illustrations

7   Porth-en-Alls by Philip Tilden.
10   St German's church c.1860.
17   Nikolaus Pevsner (1902–83).
18   An early promotional poster for Cornwall.
18   Jacket for the first edition of the *Buildings of England: Cornwall* (1951).
20   Jacket for the revised edition of the *Buildings of England: Cornwall* (2014).
21   Jacket for *Manchester* by Clare Hartwell (2000).
22   The Pevsner Architectural app.
24   Marriott's Shaft, South Wheal Frances at Carn Brea.
25   St Wyllow, Lanteglos-by-Fowey.
26   Roscarrock, St Endellion.
27   St Philip and St James, Maryfield, Antony, (1864–71) by William White.
27   All Saints, Killigrew Street, Falmouth, (1877–90) by J.D.Sedding.
29   Jubilee Pool, Battery Road, Penzance.
32   Collection of stones at the west end of Gulval church.
33   Photogrammetric images of the Gulval base.
34   Examples of the different early Cornish cross types.
35   The Evangelist Mark, with his symbolic lion at his feet.
36   The portrait of the Evangelist Mark.
37   Early medieval cross-bases in Cornwall.
38   Reconstruction of a cross in the Gulval base.
41   St Morwenna, Morwenstow.
42   The south door at Morwenstow.
43   Kilkhampton, St James, capital to the south door carved with pinecones.
44   Detail of the central arch of the north nave arcade at Morwenstow.
45   Morwenstow, detail of capital, east end of the north nave arcade.
46   The south door at St James, Shebbear (Devon).
50   Beer stone architectural fragments from Glasney; moulding profiles from Glasney; profiles of the vault ribs of the Lady Chapel and choir, Ottery St Mary;

	mouldings from Exeter Cathedral's west front and Sherborne Abbey cloister.
53	Comparative plans of the eastern ends of major churches in the diocese of Exeter:Launceston Priory.
54	Launceston Priory. General views of the moulded stonework.
54	Launceston Priory: the high altar and the screens at Ottery and Christchurch.
59	Window tracery – Exeter Cathedral, west window; St Ive; Sheviock; South Hill; St Germans; Tywardreath; St Michael Penkevil.
60	Internal detail– tomb niches at St Ive and South Hill; details of the sedilia at St Ive; sedile at St Germans; niche flanking east window, St Ive, with finial and shaft of the tomb of Bishop Stapledon in Exeter Cathedral.
61	Exeter-style sculptures with tubular-folded draperies – Exeter Cathedral south porch; Landkey; Arlington; St Ive.
66	Coloured illustration from *The Natural History of Cornwall*.
67	Plan of bridge in 1852, prior to the first widening scheme.
68	Watercolour drawing showing the proposed widening of the central arches of the bridge in 1818.
69	The second widening of the bridge in 1963.
71	Cross-section showing the original bridge sandwiched between the two widening schemes.
71	Bridge as seen from downstream on a high tide.
75	In the north (Arundell) aisle at Gwinear.
76	St Petroc, Padstow.
77	St Petroc's, Padstow. Detail of interior window arch of possible Nanfan chantry.
78	Detail of external carving at Lanlivery church c.1460s.
79	St Torney, North Hill 1500s south aisle.
80	The panelled porch at St Sidinus at Sithney.
84	Mount Edgcumbe. An exemplar of Tudor design principles.
85	An 18th-century watercolour by George Sheppard showing the east front of Trerice.
86	The Gatehouse with Lanhydrock House beyond.
87	Godolphin House, near Helston, the north front and colonnade.
88	The north front of the house at Antony.
90	Saunders Hill, Padstow.
95	The Blue Drawing room at St Michael's Mount.
95	West end of Werrington church showing Gothic detailing.
96	Engraving by Thomas Allom of Mount Edgcumbe showing 18th century Gothic detailing to the outside of the central hall.
97	Caerhayes Castle an exemplar of Picturesque Gothic.
98	Moorswater Lodge, Liskeard.
100	St Mary's church, Par.
101	Duchy Nursery, café and shop, Lostwithiel.
103	Father George Metford Parsons.
105	The parish church of St Carantoc, Crantock.
106	Lady chapel south: marriage of Mary and Joseph.

107	North nave: Saints Carantoc and Patrick.
108	South nave: the legend of St Carantoc.
109	Chancel east: Christ in Majesty.
114	The Humphrey Gryll's Monument in Helston.
115	Trevarno, a classically inspired country house near Sithney.
116	St John's church, Treslothan.
117	St Peter's, Flushing. Exterior.
117	St Peter's, Flushing. Interior.
118	Pencarrow House near Bodmin.
119	Tregrehan House, St Blazey.
121	Colonel Charles Lygon Cocks (1821–85).
122	Treverbyn Vean from the south east.
123	'The Bower of Calm Delight', Treverbyn Vean.
124	The Drawing Room, Treverbyn Vean.
126	The Dining Room, Treverbyn Vean.
127	Bishop Millman's tomb, Calcutta.
131	J P St Aubyn's signature foot-scraper, church of St John the Baptist, Penzance.
132	St Stedyana's church, Stithians: north aisle window opening.
133	South aisle baptistery window at Stithians.
134	St John the Baptist, Penzance. South-east corner.
134	St John the Baptist. Penzance.
137	St Odulph's church in Pillaton, east Cornwall.
138	St Kayna's church at St. Keyne, near Liskeard, hole in roof after masonry fall.
139	Damage to the historic fabric at Pillaton.
139	Plaster boss, recovered and re-sited in the nave at Pillaton.
140	Two church pinnacles at Pillaton after completed restoration programme.
141	Early work on St Kayna's at St Keyne. The pinnacle was completed blown clear of the tower.
142	Detail of missing pinnacle at St Kayna from the tower.
144	Completed repairs at St Kayna.

Fig. 1 *St German's church c.1860.* National Trust/ Lanhydrock.

Introduction

Paul Holden

Nikolaus Pevsner's first edition of *Cornwall* was harsh on the county – at times it was rude, often it appeared disparaging and above all it was distinctly selective. It was this, in part, that enforced a long, intense and public rivalry between Pevsner and the poet John Betjeman, who unkindly referred to his adversary as 'that dull pedant from Prussia'.[1] More conflict arose from the way which each man experienced architecture, Pevsner as a methodical and intellectual study of mass and form and Betjeman within the wider lyrical context of spirit of place. Our conference respected both views in equal measure. Hence, the papers presented here represent a considered view of the meticulous academic study of architecture, as seen in the recent published revision of *Buildings of England: Cornwall* by Peter Beacham and Nikolaus Pevsner, and the quintessence of Cornwall and Cornishness as portrayed in the expressive works of Betjeman.

The opening chapters in these proceedings by Charles O'Brien and Peter Beacham consider Pevsner and his legacy, both nationally and regionally. Nikolaus Pevsner (1902–83) arrived in England from Germany in 1934. It was during the Second World War and inspired by Georg Dehio's *Handbuch der deutschen Kunstdenkmäler* (Handbook of German Cultural Monuments)[2] that he pitched the concept of similar English architectural guidebooks to Penguin Books. Work on *Cornwall* (the first in the series) commenced in 1948 and within three years it was published. Such haste understandably led to omissions and inaccuracies, a point that Candida Lycett Green, John Betjeman's daughter, demonstrated perfectly when she recalled her father's first edition which was 'littered with notes in the margin … like "absolute balls", "what?" or "wrong" underlined'.[3] It would be nice to think that, like Betjeman, we could all follow in the age-old tradition of marking up our own copies for future reference! Such imprecisions in the first edition however are perhaps forgivable when considering how astonishing Pevsner's output was; indeed between 1951 and 1974, on average two volumes a year were published. Furthermore, the escalation of architectural history as an academic discipline during the second half of the 20th century saw revised editions appearing within his lifetime. *Cornwall*'s revision was slow to appear but its recent arrival marks a radical re-appraisal of Pevsner's work in the light of the subsequent burgeoning of understanding about the built environment and its setting.

It is fair to say that Pevsner was not an expert on early medieval sculpture and as such did not extol the real wonder of Cornish crosses, beyond their being cherished monuments and an important part of Cornish identity. Peter Beacham has gone some way towards rectifying this oversight, although unfortunately Ann Preston-Jones and Elisabeth Okasha's book *Corpus of Anglo-Saxon Stone Sculpture* arrived too late to inform his research.[4] The next three chapters focus on the medieval period, the first by Preston-Jones revealing the story behind an unusual cross-base at Gulval, dating probably from the mid to late 11th century.

This cross base, carved from a roughly square block of granite, features zoo-anthropomorphic images of the Evangelists on its four sides, their identity indicated by minute inscriptions on the Gospel books that they hold. Although it is unique in Cornwall and without direct parallel elsewhere, links can nonetheless be made with stones in the Midlands, the north of England and in Ireland which, in turn, highlights the wide range of cultural connections present in Cornwall during the 11th century. But the detail of the carving – remarkable in granite – shows that the closest parallels can be drawn with manuscripts from Brittany. The chapter goes on to discuss a possible connection with the diocesan centre in Exeter and how the granite base sits in context and relation to other early stone sculpture in Cornwall.

Alex Woodcock takes us from the west of Cornwall to the north coast, to the church of St Morwenna and St John the Baptist at Morwenstow – a church famous for its association with the eccentric 19th century vicar, the Reverend R.S. Hawker. Less well-known perhaps is its concentrated collection of 12th-century architectural sculpture, much of it in exceptional condition. Varieties of chevron, beakheads, geometric motifs and unidentifiable creatures congregate around the south door and upon the arcade of the north nave aisle. Some of this work displays close similarities with that in other sites nearby, including the church of St James at Kilkhampton and, in north Devon, the churches of Shebbear, Buckland Brewer and Woolsery. Morwenstow, however, is unique among them for its combination of Cornish and Devonian Romanesque styles and forms. Dr Woodcock's research explores the work that remains, its wider sculptural contexts, and what it might be able to tell us about the production and patronage of stone carving in the south west during the 12th century.

An emerging theme, at this early stage, is that some of the earliest sculptural work in Cornwall was ambitious, a point often overlooked by its dismissal as primitive because of the isolation of the county. John Allan takes this theme forward to the early 14th century when the prevailing architectural style was Decorated Gothic. Again, the idea that the quality of works undertaken in this style was very modest is misleading because an unusually high proportion of the major commissions have been lost, and some of the surviving examples are either sadly damaged or so massively restored that it is difficult to determine their original form.

The detailed study of architectural fragments excavated in recent years from major sites, notably the Cornwall Archaeological Unit's projects at Launceston priory and Glasney college, have recovered clear evidence of delicate and richly-carved work of a higher order than almost anything surviving above ground in the county. Some of this material is clearly related, both in its geology and in its carving style, to early 14th-century work at Exeter cathedral, while some mouldings from Glasney match those in buildings attributable to William Joy, one of the most gifted master masons working in the west at the time. In the chapter by John Allan, it is proposed that further churches in the county, notably those of St Germans (Fig.1), St Ive, St Michael Penkevil and Sheviock, form part of the same group of commissions linked to the workshop of Exeter cathedral.

Pevsner was not completely blind to medieval architectural treasures; indeed he described the seventeen-arched stone bridge built across the river Camel in north Cornwall, as 'one of the best medieval bridges in England'.[5] Built to connect the parishes of St Breock and Egloshayle during the reign of Edward IV, the first Yorkist king, Wade-Bridge later gave its name to the town which developed beside it during the 18th century. Andrew Langdon brings the story of this structure to life, drawing both on historical evidence and on living memory, with particular relevance to such current issues as river-silting and bridge widening. Widening schemes for the medieval bridge have not been without controversy; of its first widening (in 1852–53), Charles Henderson wrote that 'the new arches diminish the depth of the cutwaters upon which the beauty of the old bridge largely depended', and A. L. Rowse was later to criticise the second widening in 1963, reporting that 'they' were 'destroying something irreplaceable'.

Wade-Bridge was built during the Wars of the Roses, a period that culminated with the Cornish uprising of 1497. Despite national turmoil and local rebellion, some of Cornwall's best Perpendicular churches were built during this period and, in consequence, the production of figurative sculpture and stained glass flourished. Good examples can be seen at Bodmin (where building accounts survive), Padstow, St Winnow, St Austell, Lanlivery, Fowey and Duloe. Furthermore, evidence such as the use of Pentewan stone and stylistic similarities linking projects and families of tradesmen suggests that the Bodmin team operated over a wide area, including west Devon. Joanna Mattingly's chapter takes us beyond the medieval period and into the Reformation to look at the rise of Perpendicular church architecture in Cornwall.

While John Betjeman loved the richness of ecclesiastical architecture in Cornwall, he also harboured a passion for the country house. He was undoubtedly a man whose preoccupation with the commonplace manifested itself throughout his work as a celebration of mundane aestheticism. The inspiration he took from the 'indeterminate beauty' of provincialism and tradition is a theme he returns to several times in his book *Ghastly Good Taste: Or, a Depressing Story of the Rise and Fall of English Architecture*. First published in 1933, *Ghastly Good Taste* was cliquey, snobbish, flippant and facetious – the very antithesis of the later, more sober approach of Pevsner.

Nevertheless, no debate on Cornish architecture would be complete without reference to Betjeman. Paul Holden embraces his spirit to explore the architecture of the Cornish country house between 1540 and 1840, and presents it as a series of contradictions – that is, both a celebration of and a diatribe on what previous commentators have alluded to as mediocrity. With Betjeman at one shoulder and Pevsner at the other, Holden looks at many examples of the Cornish gentry's country seats, assessing various architectural styles and design principles deployed for wealthy Cornish patrons by national and local architects, and questioning whether the houses they built were fashionable or obscure, unique or unexceptional, progressive or retrospective.

Patrick Newberry's chapter takes this theme one stage further in summarising the long-running debate over whether there was a Gothic Revival at all in Cornwall, as opposed to a fluctuating survival of Gothic traditions. In his 1870s treatise, Charles Eastlake articulated the view that the art form died and was revived. By contrast, Kenneth Clark in his seminal work *The Gothic Revival* (1928) explored the theories of 'survival versus revival' and, notwithstanding the title of his essay, eventually gave some credence to 'survival'. This in turn was built on by Howard Colvin in the late 1940s, establishing the now more commonly held view that Gothic never actually went away.

An initial review of the evidence suggests that Cornwall was initially a repository of Gothic survival but, notwithstanding the extension of the Gothic into the 17th century as evidenced at Lanhydrock and Trewan, 18th century Cornish examples of the Gothic style of William Kent and Horace Walpole are relatively few. In the 19th century however, when national architects, such as John Loughborough Pearson, George Gilbert Scott and George Edmund Street, together with more locally-based designers such as Richard Coad, Henry Rice, James Piers St Aubyn, William White and George Wightwick, practised their Gothic skills across the county, Gothic buildings feature more strongly in Cornish architecture.

The next three chapters focus on the wider ramifications of the Gothic tradition in Cornwall. Firstly, Michael Swift investigates the restoration of St Carantoc parish church by Fr. George Metford Parsons, one of the most ambitious Anglo-Catholic restorations of the late Victorian period in Cornwall. Swift places the scheme for the stained glass windows within the architectural and liturgical context of the church, and also examines the relationships between Parsons' scheme and that of Bishop Benson for the windows of his new Truro Cathedral. Secondly, Rosamund Reid looks at the life of the compelling, energetic, entertaining and idiosyncratic architect George Wightwick (1800–72), a man described in an obituary in the *Western Daily Mercury* as 'an architect of much ability and a man of exquisite taste'. After six months working for John Foulston in Plymouth, Wightwick developed his own practice and extended his interests into Cornwall, building up a considerable network both professionally and socially on both sides of the Tamar. His work features prominently in the new *Cornwall*. Thirdly, Jeremy Pearson presents a study of the connoisseur and builder Charles Lygon-Cocks (1821–85) who built a small Gothic manor for himself at Treverbyn Vean, near Liskeard, between 1858 and 1862. Although George Gilbert Scott, assisted by Henry Rice and Richard Coad, are credited as the architects, and William Burges, architect of the remodelled parts of Cardiff Castle and Castell Coch in Wales, helped with the interior, there is little doubt that the owner designed some elements himself. This chapter draws on hitherto unpublished images of the exteriors and interiors of this spectacular house.

The establishment of a new diocese of Cornwall in 1876 and the decision to build a new cathedral in Truro was followed by the establishment of an open competition to determine a design. Amongst those who entered was the Cornish architect James Piers

St Aubyn, whose uninspired design was not shortlisted for further consideration. History has not treated St Aubyn well and despite his astonishingly high workload he has been considered in recent times as being a destroyer of church interiors rather than a restorer. Michael Warner's chapter 'Goth or Vandal' re-appraises St Aubyn's place and status within the context of the Victorian restoration of Cornwall's existing Anglican churches, together with the programme of new church building that was underway at the same time. Canon Warner argues that St Aubyn's restoration work was limited by two main factors – the first being the poor structural condition of Cornwall's Anglican churches and the second, the financial considerations of the parishes when considering restoration of their old church, or building anew.

Architectural historians can be quite unforgiving, as the case of St Aubyn proves. Rarely does conservation or restoration get the credit it deserves, so the last chapter by Simon Crosbie of Le Page Architects relates to the restoration of two damaged church towers. In January 2013 a devastating lightning strike damaged St Odulph's Church in Pillaton. Astonishingly one year later, almost to the day, another direct strike hit St Keyna in Liskeard. Le Page Architects were commissioned to undertake systematic stabilisation and restoration of these historic Grade I and 2★ listed buildings and led a team of engineers, stonemasons and contractors on the projects to repair and reconstruct the internal and external fabric of the buildings. Ironically, the north-east tower pinnacles of both churches were completely destroyed; the extensive restoration projects which ensued encompassed work on the stonework, roof trusses, roof coverings and interior fabric of the churches, all of which had been severely damaged by falling debris and yet required different methods to repair.

The emerging theme throughout this volume is one both of continuity and change. Despite constant transformation, what prevails is Cornwall's *genius loci*, a sense of place that has long been celebrated by artists, poets and writers, one of whom is Betjeman. Each chapter shows how the Cornish landscape has been shaped by the built environment and how building ambitions have been tempered by innovation, revival and popular taste in architectural design. Today, expansion and the need to build more homes have put considerable pressure on the county's natural resources, nowhere more evident than on the coast. Betjeman himself was so concerned about the number of inappropriate buildings littering the headlands that he wrote '[one] consolation [is] that no one yet has discovered how to build houses on the sea'.[6] Yet amongst the general mediocracy are examples of exhilarating design. Porth-en-Alls (Philip Tilden, 1910–14), 'a remarkable design of great originality', at Prussia Cove (ills. on p.7) and the 'simple and direct, innovatively composed' Chapel Point (John Campbell, 1935–38) at Mevagissey display clearly that good design and landscape setting can make for good bedfellows. Such examples are given prominence in the new *Cornwall*, thereby creating a painstaking record of the richness of the county's architectural legacy set alongside its art, culture and setting.[7] In her review of *Cornwall*, Candida Lycett Green wrote 'Not only is [Beacham] a lyrical and sometimes funny writer with a true gift for evoking place, but he also cares passionately about the architecture and about doing full justice to Cornwall'.[8] The essays presented here are not only a celebration of the new Cornwall but proof indeed that Pevsner and Betjeman can co-exist after all.

Notes

1. Candida Lycett Green (ed.), *John Betjeman Letters*, vol. ii, p.23 (London, 1995). Betjeman to James Lees Milne: 26 March 1952. The poet coldly referred to the art historian as 'windy', 'Granny' and 'Herr-Professor-Doktor'.
2. Dehio's guides first appeared in 1900.
3. Candida Lycett Green, 'Ultimate Guide to Cornwall', *Spectator*, 19 July 2014.
4. Ann Preston-Jones and Elisabeth Okasha, *Corpus of Anglo-Saxon Stone Sculpture, XI, Early Cornish Sculpture* (Oxford, 2014).
5. Pevsner (1951), pp.216–17.
6. John Betjeman, *Cornwall: A Shell Guide* (London, 1934), p.9.
7. Pevsner (2014), pp.463 and 353.
8. Lycett Green (2014), *Ibid*.

A Brief History of the Pevsner Architectural Guides[1]

Charles O'Brien

Nikolaus Pevsner (1902–83) (Fig.1) was born in Leipzig, Saxony, and pursued his studies in the history of art, completing his PhD in 1924. After four years as Assistant Keeper at Dresden Gallery he joined the academic staff at the University of Gottingen where he took a particular interest in Italian Mannerist and Baroque painting and later developed an enthusiasm for 20th century German architecture. With the ascendancy of Adolf Hitler in 1933 his Russian-Jewish ancestry led to his dismissal from his academic position which fuelled his decision to leave Germany for Britain, a country he first visited as a child in 1913 and to which he had returned in 1930 in pursuit of research for a series of lectures he had been asked to prepare by the University on English art and architecture.

In the period immediately after the war attitudes towards specialist publishing changed as readers' horizons widened. The ensuing rise in the demand for books was enthusiastically seized upon by Penguin Books whose output began to cover progressive and diverse subjects such as modern architecture and town planning. Two of Pevsner's contributions to this ever-expanding canon were *An Outline of European Architecture* (1942), partly prepared whilst interned at the beginning of the war and becoming one of Penguin's most successful non-fiction titles, and part of the King Penguin series *Leaves of Southwell* (1945) which was a learned analysis of the remarkable naturalistic late-13th century carved foliage on the capitals of Southwell Minster's Chapter House.

Prompted by the continuing success of the Penguin brand Allen Lane, Director of Penguin Books, invited Pevsner to suggest new publishing projects of which he had two proposals: the first was for a multi-volume scholarly history of art and architec-

Fig. 1
Nikolaus Pevsner (1902–83).
Pevsner Architectural Guides/Yale University Press

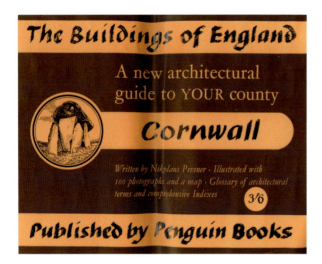

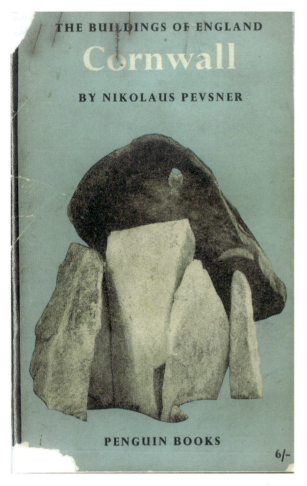

ture, which became the Pelican History of Art, the other was for a series of guidebooks of English architecture, inspired by Georg Dehio's *Handbuch der deutschen Kunstdenkmäler* a topographical inventory of Germany's important historic buildings.

The significance of such a proposal at this time was that England lacked architectural guidebooks written from the viewpoint of a European art historian. Scholarly inventories produced by official bodies – such as the Royal Commission, the Survey of London and the Victoria History of England all begun around 1900 were neither complete (Cornwall having just one volume published in 1906), nor comprehensive, nor easily portable. Popular amongst the new breed of car-driving metropolitan tourists were the Shell guide series, edited by John Betjeman of which thirteen had been published by 1939. These were neither learned or serious books which took great pleasure in commonplace characteristics of the small town such as the antiquarian past or the picturesque vistas, with much emphasis being placed on biographical or anecdotal details.[2]

It is remarkable that for the great majority of the *Buildings of England* series Pevsner managed to carry out all the fieldwork and writing himself, only later as the burden of work threatened future progress was the work shared with others or, as on two occasions, handed over to another author. Penguin provided him with an office and a secretary. The offices were in a succession of buildings in Bloomsbury, convenient for the British Museum Library and Birkbeck College where Pevsner obtained his first academic post during the war as a lecturer and later Professor of History of Art (a field of study which before the war was unrepresented in universities: the history of architecture was taught only to architectural students and concentrated on the classical tradition).

Work began on the series in 1947 – the first county selected was Cornwall (Fig.2). In these early days Pevsner employed two German secretaries to prepare his research notes, probably like himself refugees deprived of their academic careers.[3] His secretaries were given a choice of counties to research so it is perhaps unsurprising to find a quintessential holiday destination as the first and most popular port of call. Middlesex and Nottinghamshire followed, the trio published together in 1951 (Fig.3).

By the mid-1950s the pattern of work was well-established. An assistant would work for around a year on each county, preparing notes from published material available in national and local libraries. Then Pevsner, armed with fat folders of notes set off to visit two counties a year during the Easter and Summer university vacations, driven, until her death in 1963, by his wife Lola to whom the Cornwall volume was dedicated and who was credited in foreword to the Northamptonshire volume (1961) as '…an overworked taxi chauffeur without limited working hours or free Sundays'. Pevsner's attempts to drive himself in Nottinghamshire had proved nearly fatal but in practical terms it would have been impossible to cover the ground without a companion or to ensure that 'I have myself seen everything that I describe with a few exceptions' hence, after 1963, he drew on the driving skills of his assistants, mostly students.

During this time Pevsner received no salary although the cost of a full-time research assistant was thankfully met by the Leverhulme Trust and others. Without this financial support and some smaller donations the series could not have survived for, although the guides gradually gained a high reputation, the books never sold in sufficiently high numbers to make money for its publishers, then or later (early print runs close to 20,000 proved a disaster, while today typically a few thousand are printed with the expectation that they will sell out in two years or so). Pevsner lobbied Penguin hard to ensure the survival of the series and offered an open-ended commitment to maintaining the series in print at a time when similar enterprises in publishing were falling by the wayside.

With a heavy workload and only four or five weeks allowed for travelling each county the work was carried out at speed, working all day for seven days a week. Pubs and hotels were used as overnight stops where the evenings were dedicated to writing up a first draft of the long day's visit, augmented by his research files and own brief scribbled notes made on the spot. These notes were especially important as he could capture his immediate impressions – an essential ingredient of the published entries and which especially, in the analysis of the longer, more complex buildings, makes the reader feel as though Pevsner is at their elbow. There was no time for socialising or leisurely wandering, as a brief note written to his office during one of his later tours makes clear, he wrote

> I should now fill the rest of this page with nice human bits, but it's no good. The journeys are just not human. To bed 11.00, 11.30 too tired even to read the paper. Up this morning at 6 to scribble, scribble, scribble. If only one could be proud of the result.[4]

The provision of a good light, table and chair was his only request: on one occasion Lola, his wife, had gone to ask for these simple requisites and explained that her hus-

Fig. 2 Opposite page, top. *An early promotional poster for Cornwall, produced by the Penguin Books marketing department.* Pevsner Architectural Guides/Yale University Press

Fig. 3 Below *Jacket for the first edition of the* Buildings of England: Cornwall *by Nikolaus Pevsner (1951).* Pevsner Architectural Guides/Yale University Press

band worked late writing, only for the maid to enquire whether he was the author of 'love stories'. Indeed so many and various were the hotels and pubs that they stayed in, by 1958 (twelve volumes in) Pevsner was writing to the *Observer* to offer advice on the proper and economical furnishing of a hotel room.

What set the *Buildings of England* series apart from previous guide books was the scholarly attention to detail. His introductory essays varied between twenty and fifty pages each a learned synopsis of the development of architecture in each county, written-up with the latest international research in mind. Compared with the volumes like the ever-popular Shell Guides the resulting *Buildings of England* volumes were terse and uncompromisingly serious. Places were arranged alphabetically in a gazetteer format, within them entries on significant buildings were organised under churches, public buildings, and for larger places 'perambulations' provided a self-guided tour for the more curious and energetic reader. There were illustrations, gathered together and arranged in chronological order of subject matter; although not very well printed. In contrast, much attention was given to the design of a compact but clearly laid out text, which was conceived by Hans Schmoller, Penguin's outstanding chief typographer. Current volumes still follow his main conventions, for example starting a paragraph in the margin to denote a new subject, the use of small capitals within the text, and the use of italic for architects' names.

Fig. 4
Jacket for the revised edition of the Buildings of England: Cornwall *by Peter Beacham and Nikolaus Pevsner (2014).* Pevsner Architectural Guides/Yale University Press

Pevsner believed passionately in what he was trying to achieve but he was modest in his claims for the books, inviting readers to contribute corrections, and accepting that further research would often necessitate his entries to be rewritten in the future. Every new volume provoked a flood of correspondence, always punctiliously acknowledged. As the enterprise became more widely known, many of these contributions came from local experts offering advice, and enthusiasts sending lists of their favourite building types – from cinemas and country railway stations to dovecotes and windmills. So even before his work was complete in 1974, Pevsner was in no doubt that revisions of his work should have begun and *Cornwall* was among a select number which were revised in 1970. The architectural historian Enid Radcliffe, who had already updated the Essex and Yorkshire: West Riding volumes (and later revised Suffolk) undertook the adjustments to *Cornwall* but as elsewhere without the benefit of revisiting the area and limited to what could be corrected from information supplied to the office. Help was at hand from Derek Simpson, an archaeologist working at the Department of Archaeology at Leicester University, who wrote a 'completely refreshed' section on pre-history and Alec Clifton-Taylor, to whom by this time Pevsner usually turned for elucidation of building materials local to each county, added a section on provincial stone and some corrections. Radcliffe did draw on the expert local eye of Michael Trinick, Regional Director for the National Trust in Cornwall, who added new gazetteer entries for which he was credited.

By the time he had completed the series Pevsner was 73 years of age. Already plans were in hand for similar surveys, to be carried out by other writers, for Wales, Scotland and Ireland, and a programme for revised editions was ensuring that the series would continue to fulfil its original purposes – the presentation of an up-to-date critical survey of all buildings of architectural importance in a form accessible to the layman and of value to the scholar.

From the early 1980s, the adoption of a new, larger format allowed for more extensive expansion, reflecting the growing interest in a multiplicity of buildings and resources for research. Bridget Cherry and Elizabeth Williamson, the series editors, began to produce revised editions that would correct, revisit and expand the original text. Progress in revising the volumes was inevitably slow, certainly in comparison with the superhuman production of the first series. This was, in part, a reflection of first, the vastly increased body of material available at local and national level that revisers had to take into account and second, the changes in England over the past thirty to forty years which have made buildings such as churches if anything harder to visit without an appointment. The books survived Pevsner's death in 1983 and continued to be published by Penguin until 2002 when the series was taken over by Yale University Press. The progress of revision since 2002 has been greatly hurried thanks to the Pevsner Books Trust and since 2011 the Paul Mellon Centre for Studies of British Art whose generous funding has supported a combination of a full-time editorial staff who double as authors and a small band of freelance architectural historians spread across England, Scotland, Wales and Ireland who have undertaken many of the revisions and new editions. Local funding too is vital in getting each volume to press, in the case of

Fig. 5
Jacket for Manchester *by Clare Hartwell (2000) in the Pevsner City Guides series.* Pevsner Architectural Guides/Yale University Press

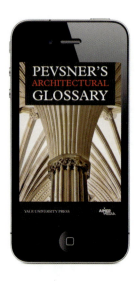

Fig. 6
The Pevsner Architectural Glossary app (2014). Pevsner Architectural Guides/Yale University Press

Cornwall support from the Tanner Trust and the Cornwall Heritage Trust has proved invaluable.

The very early volumes were cheap paperbacks. The hardback volume revisions are better produced, with high quality illustrations including colour photographs and, a larger number of text figures and maps (Fig.4). They are good books for the library, but their size makes them more awkward to carry, and their price puts them beyond the reach of many people. It is important that we should not lose sight of Pevsner's ideal of the series as an educational tool for a wide and varied readership. With that in mind, and following initial forays into paperbacks with London Docklands and City Churches (both 1998), in 2000 the Pevsner Architectural Guides diversified with a series of City Guides covering each of the major English cities where the extent of change since Pevsner's day was most acute (Fig.5). The work was supported by the Heritage Lottery Fund and English Heritage which went some way in keeping the price below £10. These guides bent some of the rules of the established series for example using integrated colour photographs and topic boxes while maintaining all of the traditional qualities of the original Pevsner guides. More recently the illustrated Architectural Glossary has been published along with an accompanying app and Twitter and Instagram feed on digital platforms. Looking ahead, spin-off volumes are to be published as introductions to, for example, churches and houses, and ultimately there is a possibility of a full digitisation of the books so that the content can be assembled in the way that users want.

In the first edition of *Cornwall* Pevsner opened his introduction with the words 'Cornwall possesses little of the highest aesthetic quality though much that is lovable and much that is moving'.[5] Perhaps his admission to underestimating the complexity of Cornwall's architectural legacy can be seen by his foreword in the 2nd edition of 1970 when he writes 'we were all beginners at the job then'. Today the Pevsner brand embraces study days at individual buildings, participation in conferences and conference proceedings and walking tours around towns (starting and ending at bookshops) which not only help with the sales of the books, but demonstrate an enduring interest in the built heritage, inspiring us to feel that our work continues to be worthwhile.

Notes

1. This text is derived from Bridget Cherry, *The Buildings of England, Ireland, Scotland and Wales: A Short History and Bibliography* (London, 1998); *The Buildings of England: A Celebration* (London, 2001); Harries, Pevsner (2011) and other information in the Pevsner Guides archive.
2. The first Shell guide of Cornwall by John Betjeman was published in 1964 by Faber & Faber.
3. In Pevsner's 1951 foreword to the first edition of *Cornwall* Dr R. Schilling is credited for 'extracting and compiling most of the facts'.
4. Private correspondence.
5. Pevsner (1951), p.11.

A Personal Reflection on Revising *Cornwall*

Peter Beacham

I shall always remember my reaction when first approached about the possibility of revising *Cornwall* – what a privilege. That feeling has never left me, and I remain more grateful than ever for the opportunity that was offered to me. For who would not relish what was on offer? The prospect of exploring a county I had known from four decades of holidays, of having an excuse to visit all its buildings worthy of inclusion in the book, and not least of meeting the people who have studied the buildings of Cornwall, lived in them, repaired them and loved them. By the end of it all, more than a decade later, I feel that I now know Cornwall better than I know Devon, a county where I have lived for nearly fifty years.

In the introduction to *Devon* W.G. Hoskins wrote

> …the writing of this book has been an immense pleasure as well as a heavy labour. It has compelled me to visit every parish, however remote, to penetrate deep lanes in search of ancient houses, to acquire a detailed knowledge of a county I thought I knew tolerably well ….. But at the end of it all I realise how little one really knows.[1]

I echo Hoskins' sentiments wholeheartedly. Revising *Cornwall* was more than an immense pleasure; it was a labour of love. It was also by far the most exacting literary task I have ever attempted, and a heavy labour that wore me down at times in the more than a decade of its doing. But most of all, even after all my journeying, observations, research, conversations and correspondence, thinking and writing, I am all too conscious of how little I still know.

I am conscious, too, of how fleeting my acquaintance with so many of Cornwall's buildings is, especially in comparison to those who have known them far more profoundly than I could ever do. Fortunately, in the true Pevsner tradition, at every turn I had every conceivable kind of help – people who did the basic research for me (the colossal mountains of material that had accumulated in the sixty years since the first edition were a major issue that had to be tackled); who shared their own research with me unstintingly; who arranged access to buildings and introduced me to owners; who

Fig. 1
Marriott's Shaft, South Wheal Frances at Carn Brea. The relict industrial of late 19th century at it's most elegaic. Pevsner Architectural Guides/Yale University Press/Eric Berry.

drove me around; and who offered me generous hospitality – without whom the book, indeed the revised series – would not have been possible. I have tried to make some small acknowledgement to the generosity of spirit I found in Cornwall in my acknowledgements in the book (my editor commented that my list of acknowledgements was unusually long!).[2]

My most profound acknowledgement remains, of course, to Nikolaus Pevsner. My admiration for the man and his achievement only grew stronger as the project progressed. Many rightly approach a Pevsner guide with something of a reverence, a perception that it is almost a sacred text that must not be tampered with. Pevsner himself did not think like that and famously regarded his first editions as a provisional attempt or, as he put it *ballons d'essai*. In his modest review of his accomplishments when completing the series with *Staffordshire* in 1974 he added '…the next round will be the revised editions … the more of these improved volumes I shall see the happier I shall be … Don't be deceived, gentle reader; it is the second editions that count'.[3] Inevitably after sixty years, much has to be added and some things radically altered but I estimate that 20% of the new edition is still the original Cornwall, especially his accounts of the medieval churches.

Rather than attempting to present a comprehensive picture of all its aspects I offer a few reflections on my approach to, and experience of, the revision. The monumental amounts of research undertaken since Pevsner visited Cornwall in the spring of 1948 were both a treasure-house of potentially relevant information, and a major logistical and intellectual challenge. I can therefore say (because I did not write them) how invaluable I consider the introductory essays by the specialist contributors were to me in shaping the book's contents: the pictures of Cornwall's geology as it presents in is building materials; of the prehistoric and medieval Cornish landscape ; of the distinctive local building traditions of the county; and of the industrial archaeology of Cornish mining and transport are all expert and admirably concise summaries of the state of our present knowledge of the subjects and form an important body of work in their own right.[4] But they are especially useful in this book because they allowed me to be highly selective about the examples of sites and buildings of these types chosen for the gazetteer. The one drawing of how a Cornish engine house works, for example, saves the need for endless repetition of what one is looking at when one encounters these structures elegiacally scattered over the Cornish landscape (Fig.1).[5]

The mention of the need for selectivity – even though this book is over four times longer than the original – highlights its core purpose and that of the series. It is not intended to be an *inventory* that is a comprehensive list of everything: to give you a few examples, it could not possibly include all the smaller houses of note in the vernacular range; nor every surviving engine house or chapel; nor even in the account of 19th century churches every restoration when there have been successive campaigns, each lasting years; or a note of every piece of Victorian stained glass. Scholarship, after all, is a fluid and progressive discipline hence the chapters that follow in this volume will undoubtedly draw on areas of scholarship not tapped into or indeed not within the scope of the new *Cornwall*. Rather the *Buildings of England* series should be seen as a succession of *guidebooks* that spur the reader on to see, appreciate, ponder – and think for themselves. As Susie Harries observed in her definitive biography *Pevsner, The Life*, 'Pevsner's objective was neither grandiose nor complicated. He simply wanted people to look at the buildings of England as they would look at any other beautiful object, not in an abstract quest for knowledge but with an everyday sense of enjoyment'.[6] And in pursuit of that objective, Pevsner readily admitted selectivity came more to the fore the nearer one came to the modern age – as does the personal judgement of the author, a significant ingredient in the success of the series. Nevertheless – and this is also very important – the author alone remains responsible for the contents.

So selectivity and concision were necessary even in my treatment of late medieval churches and many of the greater houses. We now know that relatively straightforward 15th and 16th century churches that adopted the common 'three hall' form (that is nave and flanking aisles) like Lanteglos-by-Fowey, may actually have been much more complex in their evolution than they appear, as Warwick Rodwell has shown in his

Fig. 2
St Wyllow, Lanteglos-by-Fowey. The typical interior of a late-15th/early-16th century Cornish church with nave and north and south aisles. Pevsner Architectural Guides/Yale University Press/Peter Curno.

Fig. 3 *Roscarrock, St Endellion. The late medieval south west range was modernised in the mid-to-late 16th century by the addition of this bay window to the chamber.* Pevsner Architectural Guides/Yale University Press/Eric Berry.

analysis of a superficially very similar church at Lanlivery, with substantial mid- to late medieval fabric surviving in what looks like a late 15th century church (Fig.2).[7] But this was only possible because of a (fortunately rare) situation in which all interior surfaces and a limited excavation were revealed during a significant repair programme. Similarly we now know that apparently uniform houses like the 'Tudor' Cotehele are also complex multi-phase buildings which, in Cotehele's case, were deliberately embellished to fulfil the Edgcumbe's antiquarian thirst for the 'medieval'. The original entry for Cotehele was less than five hundred words, the current entry well over 2,000, including a plan. Many of Cornwall's greater houses such as Godolphin, Lanhydrock, St Michael's Mount and Trewithen, along with some of its smaller ones like Menabilly, Roscarrock (Fig.3) and Trerice have benefitted from modern comprehensive research and investigation to show their evolution over several centuries. Summarising the contemporary understanding of such buildings is not an easy task: the original Godolphin entry, for example, was less than two hundred words, and I struggled to bring in the new entry in below 2,000.

Another major theme of the book is the importance of the Gothic Revival in Cornwall which I have attempted to illustrate in both its ecclesiastical and secular expressions. There are very interesting reasons why this movement took such a hold here, one important one being the impetus behind the Anglican church's attempt to re-invent itself in a part of the then Diocese of Exeter that had long been neglected and where Methodism was effectively the established religion: it chimed with Cornwall's wider attempt to re-invent itself during and after the collapse of mining. Another, and connected, reason was the fact that some of the pioneers of the Revival began their careers in Cornwall, with George Edmund Street at St Mary the Virgin, Par (1848) and William White at St Michael's and All Angels, Baldhu (1847–8) and the wonderful St Philip and St James, Maryfield (1864–71) (Fig.4). White's work at St Columb Major included the sublime, now sadly neglected, Victorian Romanticism of the Old Rectory (1851) and the Venetian Gothic of the St Columb Bank (1856–7). Patrick Newberry admirably teases out more about the Gothic movement later in this volume.

A fresh look at the achievements of the Victorian church restorers, often so maligned in the past, was another important theme of the book. The most important architectural dynasty in Cornwall from the second half of the 19th century to the first two decades of the 20th were the Seddings – John Dando Sedding, his elder brother, Edmund, and Edmund's son, Edmund Harold (Fig.5). All were highly skilled in Arts and Crafts Gothic and together worked on sixty-five churches which included many exemplary restorations using local materials and employing the most skilled craftsmen such as the firm of wood carvers founded by Violet Pinwill.[8] The high point of the

Fig. 4
St Philip and St James, Maryfield, Antony, (1864–71) by William White.
The chancel of one of the finest Gothic Revival churches in Cornwall.
Pevsner Architectural Guides/Yale University Press/Peter Curno.

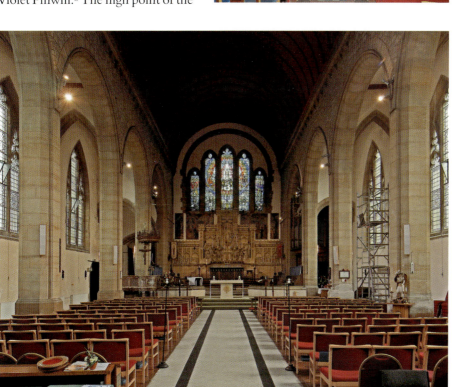

Fig. 5 *All Saints, Killigrew Street, Falmouth, (1877–90) by J.D.Sedding.*
Nave and chancel of one of his best churches with exceptionally good stained glass and carved wood work by local firms.
Pevsner Architectural Guides/Yale University Press/Eric Berry

Gothic Revival, and symbolic of Cornwall's 19th century reassertion of its separate, distinct identity, is, of course, John Loughborough Pearson's masterful cathedral in Truro.

The Seddings also represent another significant theme of 19th and 20th century Cornwall, the emergence of talented local architects such as James Hicks at Redruth, Otho B. Peter at Launceston, Henry Rice at Liskeard and Silvanus Trevail, almost omni-present. It continues into the 20th century with Captain Frank Latham the Borough Engineer of Penzance who designed Jubilee Pool in 1935 (Fig.6), and with the County Architect's Department work of the 1960s and 70s. The output of these Cornish architectural practices is an important component of the architecturally diverse character of Cornwall's exceptionally interesting historic towns, almost all of them remarkably intact – and actually in terms of their buildings and how they relate to the evolution of their morphology very little studied. In my estimation, the urban buildings of Cornwall are an almost untouched rich resource for future research.

I would like to conclude with what in many ways is the most pervasive new contribution which I have tried to offer throughout the book, and in many ways the most difficult task – the evocation of a sense of the spirit of place, character and atmosphere, something of the personality of Cornwall. The spirit of place is having something of a revival at present, most recently in Philip Marsden's *Rising Ground*. As Charles O'Brien explained in the last chapter when Pevsner first embarked on the *Buildings of England*, the main competition was seen as the *Shell Guides*, conceived by John Betjeman and John Piper in the early 1930s: it is indeed in counties like Cornwall – which in Pevsner's own phrase 'have much to reward the picturesque traveller, the archaeologist and antiquarian' that the contrast between the two series is most apparent, especially in the latter's success in conveying atmosphere.[9] Pevsner was not, of course, immune to the power of the *genius loci*: at St Day, for example, he observed that 'the church looks over a landscape of deserted tin mines with their chimneys like so many monuments to the passing of human achievement, more deeply moving than the architectural picturesque mementoes in 18th century gardens'.[10] Indeed he admired writers like Betjeman who could evoke atmosphere, and even quoted the poet verbatim when at a loss how to describe Polperro, a town omitted from the first edition because it has no individual building of special merit, 'Polperro' wrote Betjeman

> is picturesque in the extreme; there are some simple Georgian houses around the harbour, and the streets are narrow and higgledy-piggledy, and from almost every cottage window orange curtains can be seen to flutter, betokening the artistic inhabitants within. There are plenty of teashops and places for buying Cornish ware, not always manufactured in Cornwall. Despite its air of sophistication, Polperro is well worth seeing.[11]

It was just that Pevsner was both conscious of the severe constraints on space in a slim paperback and aware that evoking a sense of place was not his forte. Betjeman, of course, made an imaginary feud with the 'Herr-Professor-Doktor' which others took up (it was not reciprocated by Pevsner). Since *Cornwall* was the prototype for both Betjeman's *Shell Guides* and Pevsner's *Buildings of England*, and since I have been a lifelong admirer of Betjeman's Cornwall, trying to convey a sense of place, a sentence or two that would inform the readers why they must visit, became a major responsibility and a very challenging task – not least because as Candida Lycett Green wrote in the *Spectator* review of the book, 'Beacham felt my dad was always siting on his shoulders'.[12]

I shall, of course, leave you to decide whether I have succeeded even in a small way. But I shall give you just one example of the challenge I faced. It is, inevitably, in view of what I have just described, of how to describe St Enodoc church, in whose churchyard Betjeman chose to be buried. Pevsner's original description was prosaic to the point of exasperation, merely noting that, 'the existence of a spire is unusual in Cornwall' – as Susie Harries has said, 'Not as unusual, surely, as the existence of a chapel in the middle of a golf course, and on this occasion Betjeman might have been justified in wanting to kick him'.[13] So you can see the stakes were high; and I chose to go for broke. I opted to open my description with a line from Betjeman's own poem *Sunday Afternoon Service in St Enodoc Church, Cornwall* (1945).

> And all things draw towards St Enodoc' wrote the younger Betjeman of his spiritual home in Cornwall and final resting place. There is indeed something quietly compelling about this unassuming medieval chapelry to St Minver sheltered behind Daymer Bay below Brea Hill and once, like St Piran's Oratory and Church, almost lost in the dunes. Even though it has a little 13th century spire, rare in Cornwall, it must still be sought out in a dip among the golf links in its tamarisk-protected churchyard.[14]

It only needs a line or two – and must most certainly not be overdone – but in my judgement the buildings of Cornwall need that kind of context. Not least because, as

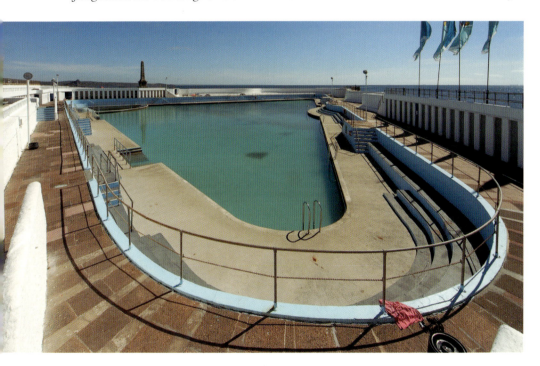

Fig. 6
Jubilee Pool, Battery Road, Penzance. An early-20th century example of the tradition of excellent buildings by a Cornish designer, here the Borough Engineer, Captain Frank Latham. Pevsner Architectural Guides/Yale University Press/Eric Berry.

Pevsner himself said in the opening line of his introduction to the original edition, 'Cornwall possesses so much that is loveable and much that is moving'.[15]

Notes

1. W.G. Hoskins, *Devon* (London, 1954), pp.xviii-xix.
2. Pevsner (2014), pp.xv-xviii.
3. Nikolaus Pevsner, *Buildings of England: Staffordshire* (Harmondsworth, 1974), p.18.
4. By Sarah Buckingham, Peter Herring, Eric Berry and John Stengelhofen respectively.
5. The drawing, on p.61, is the work of John Stengelhofen.
6. Harries, *Pevsner* (2011), p.389.
7. Warwick Rodwell, 'Lanlivery church: its archaeology and architectural history', Cornish Archaeology, 32, (1993), pp.76–111.
8. Edmund Harold Sedding and Violet Pinwell repaired the exquisite screen at St Buryan church in 1910.
9. John Betleman, *Cornwall* (London, 1964). Pevsner (1951), p.11
10. Pevsner (1951), p.148.
11. Pevsner (1970), p.142.
12. Candida Lycett Green, *The Spectator*, 19 July 2014, p.36.
13. Harries, *Pevsner* (2011), p.410.
14. Pevsner (2014), p.534.
15. Pevsner (1951), p.11.

'A large block of granite' or a unique piece of sculpture?

Ann Preston-Jones

Instead of focusing on the collection of stones that makes up a building, the subject of this chapter is one stone only. Situated in the churchyard at Gulval in west Cornwall is a large cross-base carved with simple figures surmounted with a lantern cross-head (Fig.1). Pevsner, who has always included stone crosses and other early carved stones in the Cornwall volume, simply wrote in the first edition 'One on S[outh] of churchyard with cable, key and interlace decoration…'[1] Far more comprehensive is Peter Beacham's entry in the new volume

> Outside the South wall of the church, l[eft] of the porch, inscribed stone. A churchyard cross-shaft, set upside down. On its front face plaitwork in the uppermost panel and the letters VN and VI in the middle and lower panels; key patterns on the sides. Alongside, a much eroded lantern cross head on a large granite block with a kneeling figure with a halo, holding a bible, on its main face.[2]

Before looking at the stone in detail, its setting needs some explanation. The name of Gulval is derived from that of the patron saint, Golvela.[3] In the medieval period, the estate that included Gulval church and its associated churchtown was Lanisley – a name containing the Cornish place-name element *lann*, which almost certainly refers to the church site and may indicate that a Christian settlement existed here from post-Roman times.[4] By the time of the Norman Conquest, the estate of *Lanisley* was in the ownership of the Bishop of Exeter, presumably by appropriation of the site of a pre-existing church and its lands.[5] Nothing is recorded of this earlier, pre-Domesday site, however.

The 'large block of granite' and the lantern cross-head were first recorded by J.T. Blight in 1856, beside the south-east entrance to the churchyard.[6] How or when they were first found is not known but, as Blight's illustration shows, they have been together since they were first recorded. Although it is extremely eroded, the ogee arches of the upper stone show it to be a fragment of a lantern cross of probable 15th century date. Because the stones are fixed together they have generally been regarded as parts of the same late medieval monument,[7] even though the base-stone does not have the sym-

Fig. 1
Collection of stones at the west end of Gulval church. Author.

Fig. 2
Opposite page Photogrammetric images of the Gulval base. These are created by taking a great many overlapping images and processing them using a filter called ambient occlusion. With kind permission of Tom Goskar (image assembled by Daniel Rose-Jones).

metrical form that might be expected of a Gothic cross-base and the angel-like figure carved on its south face is unlike most late medieval angels, such as those on the capitals and font in Gulval Church.

The first to recognise that this stone might be much earlier than 15th century were Mick Aston and Teresa Hall,[8] who suggested that far from being part of a Gothic monument, the stone might be a large cross-base of late 9th- or early 10th-century date, its nearest parallels being in Ireland and Northumbria.

Their suggestions provoked a reassessment of the stone, starting with full photographic recording of all four sides, including those up against the church walls which are normally invisible. Importantly, the record was enhanced with 3D photogrammetric recording by Tom Goskar (Fig.2).[9] This reassessment concluded that the base-stone was likely to have been carved a few decades either side of the Norman Conquest and, in the context of other Cornish sculpture of the period, is extremely unusual.[10] To appreciate this, it is important to understand the nature of early medieval sculpture in Cornwall; by 'early medieval' I mean the period up to and including the early decades of the Norman Conquest – that is up to about 1200.

There are no certain surviving buildings of pre-Norman date in Cornwall, where the most conspicuous remains of the period between the departure of the Romans and the establishment of Norman rule are the carved stones (Fig.3). The early Christian memorial stones belong to the immediately post-Roman period and date broadly to the late 5th to 7th centuries. After this, there is a gap in the record before the sculptured crosses first appear, towards the end of the 9th century.[11] One of the earliest is the Doniert Stone (Fig.6a, b), a pedestal for a cross which would have been socketed together in sections, and can be reasonably closely dated from its inscription commemorating the last known Cornish king.[12] After this, there is a continuous sequence of cross-carving in Cornwall throughout the medieval period.

These early crosses are decorated with interlace, knotwork, key patterns and plant scrolls and can be categorised into three main groups, examples of which can be seen in Fig. 3.[13] However, unlike these, the carving on the Gulval base is of four individual large figures, all with haloes and holding books. There is some writing on at least two of the books. Three face sideways, with only the angel-like figure facing forwards. The folds of their clothing can be seen, and in three cases, the figures are crouching – per-

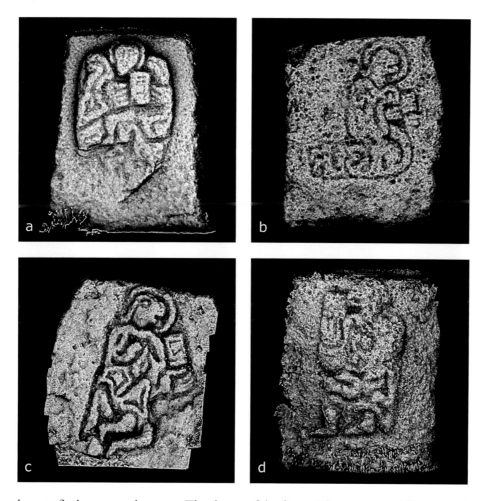

haps to fit them onto the stone. The shapes of the figures' faces are especially unusual, with three being distinctly animal-like: b has a mouth shaped like a muzzle, while d is distinctly beak-like. The only one that looks slightly human is the angel. Considering that the carving is cut in very coarse-grained Land's End granite, a remarkable amount of detail can be seen.[14]

Although they appear unusual, the explanation for these forms is that they are zoo-anthropomorphic (half man, half animal) images of the Four Evangelists: Matthew, Mark, Luke and John, arranged clockwise around the stone.[15] The origin of this symbolism is found in the bible, in Revelation 4, verses 6–7:

> And before the throne there was what looked like a sea of glass, like unto crystal: and in the midst of the throne, and round about the throne, were four beasts...
> And the first beast was like a lion, and the second beast was like a calf, and the third beast had a face as a man, the fourth beast was like a flying eagle.

Fig. 3 *Examples of the different early Cornish cross types: a. Long Cross, St Endellion, an example of an inscribed memorial stone with Chi-Rho, of probable 6th-7th century date; b. St Neot, 'panelled interlace' group; c. Cardinham, mid Cornwall foliage-decorated group; d. Lanherne, Penwith group, with Crucifixion on one side of the head and five bosses on the reverse; e. Lanivet 2, cross with incised decoration, probably of the transitional period between early and later medieval periods. The very much simpler wayside crosses, a common feature in Cornwall, are thought to belong to the 12th and 13th centuries, while lantern crosses belong to the 15th and 16th.* Author (image assembled by Daniel Rose-Jones).

Hence the Evangelists may be represented as the four creatures: Matthew as a man, Mark as a lion, Luke as a stylised calf and John an eagle. This symbolism can be seen in many early British manuscripts. For example, in the Book of Kells, the Evangelists are portrayed as animals.[16] In the Lindisfarne Gospels, the Evangelists are depicted as human figures, with their symbolic animals close by.[17] This symbolism continued in use throughout the medieval period so that, whether by coincidence or design, Evangelists as human figures accompanied by their representative creatures can be seen carved in stone on the tower of Gulval Church (Fig.4).

From here it could be an easy step to combining both forms to create the half animal, half human, zoo-anthropomorphic figures like those seen in the Leofric Gospels and the Harkness/Landévennec Gospels.[18] Both books were written and illuminated in Brittany in the late 9th or early 10th centuries. In illustrations in the Leofric Gospels, the Evangelist is also named on his gospel book (Fig.5). With this interpretation in mind it becomes apparent that the image on the front face is in fact Matthew, as a winged man. His face, surrounded by its halo, can be clearly seen, and in his hands is his gospel book which carries an abbreviation of his name – MT – incised on the front.

Moving clockwise around the stone, the next image is of Mark, his face framed by a massive halo. As a man with lion's head, the muzzle-like profile is explained while the rather thick neck and curled hair may represent the mane. Some markings on the book could be letters from the name Mark, but this is uncertain.

The identity of the third figure as Luke is in no doubt since the letters LS, for 'Lucas', are cut clearly on the cover of his book. Since Luke is a calf, the curved line behind the eye may perhaps represent a curled horn. It is even possible to see the creature's tongue, lolling from its mouth.

The last figure is John, the eagle. Unfortunately, this is the most worn of the carvings but nonetheless the shape of the head, with its curved beak, is obvious. He holds his book aloft but due to erosion, the existence of lettering is not clear.

Evangelists depicted as human figures with the animal heads of their symbols are relatively common in early Breton manuscripts. An example can be seen on the title page of the Landévennec Gospels.[19] Here, as on the Gulval stone, the Evangelists each hold their books and all have their heads in profile except Matthew, the man, who faces forward. Mirroring the passage in Revelation, the Evangelists are set around a central figure identified by the letters IHC XPS on his book, an abbreviation of 'Jesus Christ' in Greek.

Fig. 4
The Evangelist Mark, with his symbolic lion at his feet: late-medieval carving on Gulval Church tower.

Many points of comparison can be seen between the Breton manuscripts and the images on the Gulval stone. For example, the very stylised form of the figures, the names on their books,[20] the curling hair, large haloes, roughly rendered drapery, angle of the heads (looking forward, tilted slightly up) and in the case of Mark and Luke, the tongue sticking out. Many differences exist as well, but the similarities nonetheless suggest a connection between the representations in parchment and stone. In the conclusion to this paper the reason for this will be considered; but first, the stone will be examined in its wider context.

It is difficult to find parallels for this base-stone and its decoration in Cornish early medieval sculpture. In terms of the figure carving, the closest parallels are with the Penwith group crosses, found in much the same area as Gulval,[21] which feature a Crucifixion on the head (Fig. 3d). Other than these, two small sketchy figures on a

Fig. 5
The portrait of the Evangelist Mark, from the Leofric Gospels at the Bodleian Library, University of Oxford, MS. Auct. D.2.16, fol. 71v.

cross at Penzance and a large incised figure on a cross at Lanivet (Fig. 3e) is the sum of figure carving;[22] although a cross dated to perhaps 1100 at Tintagel has an inscription naming Matthew, Mark, Luke and John and four tiny heads between the arms on the cross-head, which may be intended to represent the Evangelists.[23]

Elsewhere, Evangelists are occasionally found in stone sculpture, but examples are rare. The best are from the north of England where, for example, a 9th century cross-shaft at Halton in Lancashire has the Evangelists, in symbolic form, arranged around the shaft; and a beautiful 11th century cross-head at Durham features the Lamb of God at the centre, with the Evangelists set around him in each of the arms.[24] Evangelists are named on two crosses in Wales,[25] but are absent from stone sculpture in Ireland.

The physical attributes of the Gulval base are likewise difficult to match closely. It is an irregular, roughly square block of granite up to 88 cm high and on average 63 by 70 cm across. Because it has been filled with cement and has the lantern head in it, the exact size of the mortice is uncertain but it is approximately 36 cm square. The top edge of the stone is rebated.

Although plenty of early crosses survive in Cornwall, there are only a few definite examples of the bases that supported them. As Fig. 6 shows, they are rather different from the Gulval stone. In shape, the Gulval base is most like the Doniert Stone. The latter currently stands higher than the Gulval base, but if the bottom, uncarved section were sunk in the ground – as it was presumably intended to be – then the visible, carved, part would be approximately the same height as the Gulval stone. Even so, the two differ in significant ways. Compared to Gulval, the Doniert Stone is far more neatly shaped and regular. It has beautifully cut and executed decoration formed within an edge moulding and the regular, geometric ornament covers the entire visible face of the stone (apart from that with the inscription). In contrast, the Gulval base has no moulding around the edge and decoration is confined to the one figure on each side.

Although parallels for this type of base are difficult to find elsewhere in the country, one or two do exist. For example, at Margam in south-east Wales is the base of a cross,

Fig. 6
Early medieval cross-bases in Cornwall: a. the Doniert Stone, inscribed face; b. the Doniert Stone, reverse, showing socket; c. Padstow churchyard, with the lower part of the cross shaft in it, seen from the side. This is a plain uncarved slab of granite; d. inscribed cross-base at Lanhadron, St Ewe. This morticed slab of Pentewan Stone has an inscription around the edge. Image assembled by Daniel Rose-Jones.

77 cm high: but with its knotwork and key patterns it is more like the Doniert Stone than Gulval.[26] On the other hand, decorated cross-bases are common in Ireland, and it is here that the best parallels for the Gulval base exist. Most have a formal, tapering shape, but some are rougher, blockier stones, like that at Killeany, County Galway.[27] A feature common to most, shared by the Gulval base, is the rebated edge around the top of the stone. This can be a prominent, formal feature of the design, or just a small lip, like Gulval's. One Irish cross pedestal, at Castledermot, County Kildare, even has a large single figure carved on it, crouched up to fit on the stone.[28]

Like the Cornish crosses, the style of Irish high crosses varies with date. Broadly, the earliest, from the late 8th century, feature intricate geometric ornament and spirals whereas slightly later monuments, like the Scripture Cross at Clonmacnoise, bear complex biblical scenes. The latest Irish crosses, dating from a revival in cross-carving of the 12th century, feature large figures of the Crucifixion, and bishops or abbots.[29] The relevance of this to the Gulval base will be considered in the conclusion to this paper. First, however, the stature and form of the cross that the Gulval base supported will be considered, starting with its likely height.

Fig. 7
Reconstruction of a cross in the Gulval base.
With kind permission of Daniel Rose-Jones

Assuming that the mortice in the stone is 36 cm across, and that the cross shaft is likely to have been stepped out from the tenon by perhaps 2–3 cm all round, then the missing cross-shaft may have measured very approximately 40–45 cm across at the bottom.[30] An early Cornish cross with a shaft of approximately 40 cm across is that at Lanhydrock, which stands 2.4 m high.[31] Lanteglos 1 and 2 (cross-shaft and head) have a shaft 45 cm wide at the base and together would have stood over 2.5 m high.[32] From these it is possible to extrapolate that the cross at Gulval stood perhaps 2.5 m high and if so, the assemblage of base and cross could have been over 3 metres in height. With its exceptional carving, it would have been one of the most impressive monuments in the area.

The type of decoration on the missing cross is difficult to determine, since the base is so different in character from any other early medieval sculpture in Cornwall. However, given that the images on the base are presented alone, with no surrounding decoration, lacking even an edge-moulding, it seems likely that the rest of the decoration was relatively sparse. It is unlikely that it featured the all-over geometric ornamentation that was popular in the 10th and first half of the 11th centuries: though incised patterns, like those on the St Levan or Penzance crosses might have existed.[33]

One thing that seems almost certain is that the cross-head had a Crucifixion. Earlier in this paper it was shown that the Gulval carvings are very similar to the zoo-anthropomorphic images of Evangelists in Breton Gospel Books. On the title page of the Landévennec Gospels, the Evangelists are set around a portrait of Christ. It therefore seems probable that an image of Christ would have been carved on the cross. The fact that the early crosses of the Penzance area generally include a Crucifixion makes this all the more likely. Gulval's Crucifixion might have resembled that shown in Fig. 3d or may alternatively have been like the much simpler stick man on the Penzance Cross, said to represent the Risen Christ:[34] but given the work that has gone into carving the base, it seems likely that the image was an impressive and large one (Fig 7).

In common with other early monuments in the area, the reverse side of the cross-head may simply have borne a carved cross, perhaps like that on the Phillack or Sancreed 2 crosses.[35] However, based on the historical context and the Irish parallels already mentioned an additional, rather more speculative, suggestion is possible.

At the outset it was noted that the original name for Gulval was Lanisley. Lanisley is recorded in Domesday Book, and the fuller Exeter Domesday tells us that in 1066 the manor was held by Bishop Leofric of Exeter, in demesne.[36] By 1086 its tenant was Roland, Archdeacon of Exeter. So in the second half of the 11th century there was a close link between Gulval and the diocese of Exeter. Leofric was a renowned collector of books and his library included a Breton Gospel book.[37] Known now as the Leofric Gospels, this still survives and contains three original Evangelist portraits – noted above for their similarities to the Gulval images (Fig. 5). So, although it is not known whether the bishop or archdeacon ever visited Gulval personally, it seems a possibility that the connection provides a context for both commissioning this impressive piece of sculpture and providing the models on which the images were based. Was a book like the Leofric Gospels used in helping to design the Gulval cross-base?

To suggest what else may have appeared on the cross, the Irish high crosses might be referred to for inspiration. Here the latest, of the 12th century, are decorated with very large, sometimes three dimensional images.[38] These images normally include a Crucifixion, but may also feature abbots or bishops, as for example at Dysert O'Dea in Co. Clare.[39] So, taking into account Gulval's close connection with the Bishop of Exeter, the resemblance of Gulval's base to Irish cross-bases, and the fact that other crosses in the area may have been influenced by Irish sculpture, the audacious suggestion is made that an image of a bishop may have featured on the missing Gulval Cross.

Notes

1. Pevsner (1951), p.63–4.
2. Pevsner (2014), p.224.
3. O.J. Padel, *A Popular Dictionary of Cornish Place-Names* (Penzance, 1988), p.91.
4. *Idem*. For discussion of the meaning of the place-name element 'lann' in Cornish place-names refer to O.J. Padel, 'Cornish Language Notes: 5, Cornish Names of Parish Churches', *Cornish Studies*, 4/5, (1976–77), pp.15–27 and O.J. Padel, 'Cornish Place-Name Elements', *English Place-Name Society*, vol. LVI/LVII, (Nottingham, 1985), pp.142–4.
5. C. Thorn and F. Thorn (eds.), *Domesday Book 10, Cornwall*, (Chichester, 1979), 2,10. N. Orme, *Cornwall and the Cross: Christianity 500 – 1560*, (Chichester, 2007), pp.10–11 and 24.
6. J.T. Blight, *Ancient Crosses and Other Antiquities, in the West of Cornwall*, (London and Penzance, 1858) p.50.
7. *Idem*. J.T. Blight, *Churches of West Cornwall; with Notes of Antiquities of the District*, (Oxford and London, 1885), pp.127. Arthur G. Langdon, *Old Cornish Crosses*, (Truro, 1896), p.426.
8. M. Aston, T. Hall, R.Cramp, A. Preston-Jones and A.G.Langdon, 'An Unusual Stone at Gulval Church, a Note', *Cornwall Archaeological Society Newsletter* No. 132, (2013) (unpaginated).
9. T. Goskar, no title, *Cornwall Archaeological Society Newsletter* No. 133, (2013) (unpaginated). Ann Preston-Jones and Elisabeth Okasha, *Corpus of Anglo-Saxon Stone Sculpture vol. XI, Early Cornish Sculpture*, (Oxford, 2013), p.7, Ills.338–41.
10. *Ibid.*, pp.147–52.
11. *Ibid.*, pp.44–7. See also Ann Preston-Jones, 'The Early Medieval Church', *Cornish Archaeology*, 50, (2011), pp.274–5.
12. Preston-Jones and Okasha, *Corpus of Anglo-Saxon Stone Sculpture* pp.134–7.
13. *Ibid.*, pp.85–95. While being distinctively Cornish, these monuments display a significant level of cross-cultural influence. 'Panelled interlace' crosses have a strong resemblance to crosses found in south Wales. The plant decoration of the mid-Cornwall group is an English, not Celtic, form of pre-Norman decoration while the use of five bosses and the Crucifixion on the Penwith group crosses may reflect Irish influence.
14. *Ibid.*, pp.147–52, Ills. 88–91 and pp.338–41.
15. *Ibid.*, pp.149–50. Tom Goskar: http://tom.goskar.com/2013/07/23/a-medieval-discovery-at-gulval-church-cornwall/;
16. Trinity College, Dublin, MS 58. The Book of Kells (AD 800) is available as an online resource at http://digitalcollections.tcd.ie/home/index.php?DRIS_ID=MS58_003v
17. British Library, MS Cotton Nero D IV. The Lindisfarne Gospels, a late 7th or early 8th century manuscript, is available as an online resource at http://www.bl.uk/turning-the-pages/?id=fdbcc772–3e21–468d-8ca1–9c192f0f939c&type=book
18. Bodleian Library MS. Auct. D.2.16. The Leofric Gospels, made at Landévennec, Brittany, late 9th or early 10th century is available as an online resource at
    http://image.ox.ac.uk/show?collection=bodleian&manuscript=msauctd216 New York Public Library: Manuscripts

and Archives Division, MSS Col 2557. The Harkness or Landévennec Gospels, of similar date, are also available as an online resource at, http://exhibitions.nypl.org/threefaiths/node/33 See also C.R. Morey, E.K. Rand, and C.H. Kraeling, *The Gospel Book of Landévennec (the Harkness Gospels) in the New York Public Library*, (Cambridge, MA, 1931) which contains examples of illustrations from other Breton manuscripts.

19. Morey et al, *Landevennec*, p.193, Fig.1.
20. Bodleian Library MS. Auct. D.2.16, fols 28v., 71v., 101v., (Leofric Gospels) the names are abbreviated differently from Gulval's: http://image.ox.ac.uk/show?collection=bodleian&manuscript=msauctd216
21. Preston-Jones and Okasha, *Corpus of Anglo-Saxon Stone Sculpture*, Fig. 21.
22. *Ibid.*, pp.77–80, Ills.189 and 190.
23. *Ibid.*, pp.201–3, Ills.225 and 358.
24. R.N. Bailey, *Corpus of Anglo-Saxon Stone Sculpture vol. IX, Cheshire and Lancashire*, (Oxford, 2010) pp.183–5, Ills.464, pp.476–9. R. Cramp, *Corpus of Anglo-Saxon Stone Sculpture vol. I, County Durham and Northumberland*, (London,1984), pp.70–71, Pl. 46. E. Coatsworth, 'The four cross-heads from the Durham Chapter House, Durham', in (ed) James Lang, *Anglo-Saxon and Viking Age Sculpture*, British Archaeological Reports British Series 49, (Oxford, 1978), p.86, Fig.1A.
25. At Llanhamlach, Breconshire, of 10th to 11th century date, see M. Redknap and J.M. Lewis, *A Corpus of Early Medieval Inscribed Stones and Stone Sculpture in Wales, I: South-West Wales*, (Cardiff, 2007), pp.210–3. At St David's, Pembrokeshire, of late 11th to 12th century date, see N. Edwards, *A Corpus of Early Medieval Inscribed Stones and Stone Sculpture in Wales, II: South-West Wales*, (Cardiff, 2007), pp.444–6.
26. Redknap and Lewis, *A Corpus of Early Medieval Inscribed Stones and Stone Sculpture in Wales*, pp.408–20.
27. P. Harbison, *The High Crosses of Ireland: an iconographical and photographic survey*, 3 vols., (Bonn, 1992), p.126, Fig.418.
28. *Ibid.*, p.38, Fig.104.
29. N. Edwards, *The Archaeology of Early Medieval Ireland*, (London, 1990), pp.168–70.
30. Note that the shaft of the churchyard cross at Gulval is not likely to have fitted into the base as its dimensions are different from those of the mortice in the base.
31. Preston-Jones and Okasha, *Corpus of Anglo-Saxon Stone Sculpture*, pp.158–9, Ills.110–5.
32. *Ibid.*, pp.164–7, Ills.131–7.
33. *Ibid.*, pp.186–8, 239–40, Ills.185–8, 307–11.
34. A.C. Thomas, *Penzance Market Cross: a Cornish Wonder re-wondered*, (Penzance, 1999), pp.42–3, Fig.19.
35. Preston-Jones and Okasha, *Corpus of Anglo-Saxon Stone Sculpture*, Ills. 200, 318.
36. *Ibid.*, p.151.
37. L. J. Lloyd, 'Leofric as Bibliophile', in (eds) F. Barlow, K. M. Dexter, A. M. Erskine and L. J. Lloyd, *Leofric of Exeter*, (Exeter, 1972), pp.32–42.
38. Edwards, *The Archaeology of Early Medieval Ireland*, pp.169–70.
39. Harbison, *The High Crosses of Ireland*, vol. 1, pp.83–6, vol. 2, Figs.261–5.

Beasts and Beakheads: Romanesque Sculpture at Morwenstow

Alex Woodcock

Romanesque sculpture combines geometric designs, monsters, animals, plants and human figures with the architectural elements of buildings, for example capitals and tympana. Flourishing in the British Isles during the late-11th and 12th centuries the often startling imagery has meant that its reception has been far from straightforward, and from the controversial origins of the term in the early 1800s to its more widespread acceptance as a legitimate style over a century later, it has had to fight battles of taste.[1] The Romanesque in Cornwall is no exception.

In *England's Thousand Best Churches* Simon Jenkins draws the reader's attention to

Fig. 1
St Morwenna, Morwenstow.
Author.

Fig. 2
The south door at Morwenstow. The weathered beakheads and chevrons indicate that the porch is a post-medieval addition, probably added when the south aisle was built and the doorway moved.
Author.

the Romanesque sculpture that survives at the church of St Morwenna in Morwenstow (Fig. 1) 'Norman beasts adorn the doorway' he writes, 'and the Norman north arcade survives, green, damp and primitive, except for two Early Gothic arches closest to the chancel'.[2] If the statement is in part incorrect – it is the carving around the south door that has developed a green patina due to its more exposed position (Fig. 2) – can we forgive the use of the word primitive? Perhaps. Nevertheless it introduces an atmosphere conducive to an unfair judgement, defined, as the word conventionally is 'in negative terms … lacking in elements such as organization, refinement and technological accomplishment' and generally used to refer to something 'less complex, or less advanced' than something else.[3] These connotations of simplicity may not have been the intention of the author; however, they are hard to ignore. On reflection, reading this statement made me realise that for some years now I have been harbouring a growing sense of the Romanesque stonecarving at Morwenstow as ambitious, bold work with a strong sense of design. Nor am I the first to think along these lines. In 1909 the architect Edmund Harold Sedding wrote that 'both for variety and skill in execution' the stonework at Morwenstow 'has no parallel in Cornwall'.[4] So, with thanks to Simon Jenkins for helping to kick-start my thinking on the subject, and bolstered by the enthusiasm of Edmund Harold Sedding, in this chapter I would like to explore in brief what survives at the church of St Morwenna and see what it may be able to tell us about architectural stonecarving in the mid to later 12th century in north Cornwall.

The Romanesque architectural sculpture of Cornwall is relatively overlooked.[5] This might be due to the lack of any one complete or near-complete site, unlike, for example, Kilpeck in Herefordshire or Alne in Yorkshire.[6] Perhaps the closest comparable example in the county is the church at St Germans which retains most of its west end, including a doorway of seven orders all carved with various forms of chevron. This has, however, weathered badly with considerable loss of detail. In general, the material in Cornwall tends to be scattered, a doorway here, a corbel or a font there, which can give the impression of uneven quality and lack of innovation. Yet to look at some of the remaining doorways of the county, for example at St Anthony-in-Roseland, or Cury on the Lizard, is to find highly original designs. At the former, the repeating foliate imagery carved into the voussoir blocks of the inner order is framed by semi-circular tracery, while at the latter, a hyphenated chevron form (a point alternating with a straight section) is used freely on the jambs of the doorway as well as to highlight the interlaced circles on the tympanum. Groups of fonts, while often repeating standard motifs, also break free of them by altering patterns or adding subtle twists to conventional designs. Those at Lanreath and Ladock, both carved with a palmette motif similar to many of those found in south Devon, do this through their development of star and other geometric designs.[7] Figure sculpture, though rare in the county, exists in Launceston at the church of St Stephen.[8]

Leaving the tub font with its cable moulding aside, there are two distinct groups of Romanesque architectural sculpture at Morwenstow. The first is around the south door and porch. This is original to the site but was moved during the 16th century when the south aisle was added. The second, that of the north nave arcade, is both original and in situ. Each area shows distinct stylistic leanings, with the work of the south

Fig. 3
Kilkhampton, St James, capital to the south door carved with pinecones. A similar pinecone capital can be found on the east side of the south door at Morwenstow.
Author.

Fig. 4
Detail of the central arch of the north nave arcade at Morwenstow to show chevrons and beakheads.
Author.

door displaying close similarities to another church nearby, that of St James at Kilkhampton, while the north arcade leans stylistically towards several north Devon doorways at Buckland Brewer, Shebbear and West Woolfardisworthy (Woolsery).[9]

With the enlargement of the church in the second half of the 16th century, the Romanesque south door at Morwenstow was moved to the outer wall of the aisle and then divided, its outermost arch used to frame the entrance to the porch itself. Entering the churchyard from the road, along the footpath that winds through the graves, this arch is the first substantial piece of 12th century sculpture that the visitor sees. Composed of frontal chevron, that is, a chevron form angled outwards towards the observer, it supports a run of randomly arranged bosses and beast masks on the outside.[10] Other carved stones are set into the exterior of this porch. At the apex, two carved beasts support the Agnus Dei on a rope or cord, the ends of which are held in each creature's mouth, and, lower down, some corbels too, animal masks whose enormous eyes are balanced by wide grins.

Inside the porch is the rest of the doorway. Here the outer arch (formerly the middle one) is carved with lateral and frontal chevron, the points of each meeting in the middle, while the inner arch features a run of weathered beakheads. Beakheads are highly distinctive animal and human masks, with, as their name suggests, a beak or other kind of mouth that appears to grip the moulding profile of the arch. The capitals are all carved and all weathered to a high degree as the door was originally unprotected. There are stylised foliage designs and on the middle capitals a double-bodied creature, a central head uniting its two bodies (west side), and on the opposite side a spray of pine cones. This latter motif can be found carved on a capital to the south door at Kilkhampton (Fig. 3) which also shares with Morwenstow the inner order of beakhead and some of the chevron styles, features that might suggest that the doors at both sites were carved by a similar team of stonemasons.

Walking into the church it is possible to identify a different style in the sculpture of the north nave arcade (Fig. 4). Of this period there are three arches supported by cylindrical columns and each arch is decorated differently. The central one is the most heavily carved, with, from inner to outer order, frontal chevron (like the doorway), beakheads and small bosses. The westernmost arch is largely plain, and the arch furthest east has, again from inner to outer, triple chevron, a plain moulding and on the outside, a geometric motif. The capital and abacus to the eastern termination of this arch are also richly carved, with large volutes to the capital, intersecting semicircles and a band of six-spoked rosette motifs along the abacus (Fig. 5).

The decoration of this arcade has numerous close stylistic similarities with sculpture only a few miles away in north Devon. As I have already mentioned there are three doorways, each of very similar character, at the churches of Buckland Brewer, Shebbear and Woolsery (Fig. 6). These doorways are almost identical, each one consisting of an inner order of triple chevron, a central band of beakheads and masks (of four distinct varieties) and an outer run of the same geometric shape that we see in the eastern nave arch at Morwenstow. The capitals to the doorways too all feature the same large volutes supporting an abacus of interlaced semicircles. These doorways are so uniform as to suggest standardised production. It's not just doorways either. The font at Hartland (Devon) displays the hallmarks of this north Devon and Morwenstow group, with intersecting semicircles, volutes, vertical chevron, and, beneath the corners, the same heads with broad moustaches that are found among the beakheads. These pieces of stonecarving suggest the presence of a group of masons producing work for different sites in the region, drawing from a repertoire of distinctive motifs.

Why Morwenstow? It appears to contain the full range of designs and motifs to be found across both north Cornwall and north Devon. What was going on in the mid-12th century in this part of the world to warrant all this rich carving in the parish churches of the area? Two things, I think, are worth a closer look. First, the civil war that followed the death of Henry I in 1135, and second, the re-establishment of Hartland Abbey as an Augustinian Priory in 1169.

After the Conquest William I gave Cornwall to his half-brother Robert, the Count of Mortain, to govern on his behalf. However, after a period of relative peace between them both Robert and then later his son William rebelled against the crown. Numerous rebellions followed until Henry I defeated the Mortains and their supporters at Tinchebrai in

Fig. 5 *Morwenstow, detail of capital, east end of the north nave arcade. These architectural motifs are repeated throughout some of the churches of north Devon.* Author.

Fig. 6
The south door at St James, Shebbear (Devon) carved with beakhead, chevron and other geometric designs similar to those at Morwenstow. Author.

1106. Henry I retained the Earldom of Cornwall for himself and, during the troubled years of the civil war that followed his death in 1135, the county became an arena in which two of his illegitimate sons built their power bases. The manor of Kilkhampton in the north of the county was owned by one of them, Robert of Gloucester, who may have built the castle there, later destroyed by Henry II.[11] We have already seen how the south door of the church of St James in Kilkhampton is one of the most significant pieces of work in the county; if Robert of Gloucester was responsible for this then he, like his father before him, appears to have been a patron of art.

Beakhead ornament is important within this context. Beakhead is typical of later Romanesque architectural sculpture. Its origin is usually considered to be Reading Abbey in Berkshire which was founded by Henry I as his mausoleum in 1121. In England beakhead predominates in Oxfordshire and Yorkshire which makes Kilkhampton and nearby Morwenstow unusual for possessing the motif. If, as Ron Baxter has written, it is 'unsuspected links of patronage' which can throw up surprisingly rich displays of beakhead ornament 'in counties that are otherwise lacking in the motif', perhaps this is what we have at Kilkhampton: a son of Henry I emulating the ambitious programmes of art of his father in an attempt, perhaps, to bolster his own power.[12] The south door at Morwenstow, so close in style to that at Kilkhampton and sharing some of its motifs, is likely to be contemporary.

Medieval churches were generally enlarged by the building of an aisle, which meant having to replace an already existing external wall with an arcade. As a result, the north nave arcade at Morwenstow may well be slightly later in date than its south door. This arcade shows close similarities with the north Devon doorways. Such a concentration of doorways, each composed of standardized elements, suggests production at a central workshop or even quarry. The north Devon doorways have been dated to between 1160 and 1180 on stylistic grounds, which makes the re-establishment of Hartland Abbey in 1169 a prime candidate for the focus of carving, and perhaps these originated from the workshops there.[13] Historical evidence does suggest close, and high status, connections. The church at Woolsery, for example, was bestowed by Hugh Peverell in the 12th century upon Hartland Abbey with the grant later confirmed by Richard I, while in the same period Shebbear was a royal manor, granted by Henry II to the one of the sons of Stephen.[14]

Despite documentary evidence, which exists from the later medieval period, it is still unclear how patronage for architectural stonecarving worked.[15] What was the source material? How did the carvers work? Just how much input into the finished design did the architect or master mason have? Architectural sculpture was part and parcel of medieval building so the designs used could have been specified by, for example, the patrons of the entire project, the patrons of a chapel or aisle, the architect, or left to the stonemason. Without written contracts or other documents establishing connections between patrons and specific motifs is largely guesswork, however, and certainly for the 12th century we are often left with the archaeological material alone. Yet the uniformity of motifs and doorways does suggest the production of standard elements that may have been carved off-site, delivered and fitted, as other sculptural material such as fonts probably were.[16]

Morwenstow, then, is an important site for the Romanesque in Cornwall, displaying a wide range of work that we can assign to the north Devon and north Cornwall group of stonemasons of the mid to late 12th century.

To conclude, characteristic of the updated edition of *Cornwall* is the acceptance of the poetic feeling inspired by the setting of many of the county's buildings. Morwenstow is rightly described as one of 'the most atmospheric of churches, even for Cornwall. Its position is incomparably romantic; the way the tower stands four-square and silent above the coombe, facing the sea beyond, is unforgettable'.[17] Sedding was similarly transfixed by, as he put it, the 'wild situation of this most charming sanctuary' and as his book attests spent considerable hours drawing the work here.[18] Certainly, standing in the church on a dark winter's afternoon, the wind loud in the trees outside, it is not difficult to feel the great elemental power of the place and perhaps the expectation of its art is that, steeped in such a situation, it is somehow 'primitive'. It's not a giant leap to make from a 'wild and romantic' setting to a 'primitive and mysterious' art. Primitive, however, opens the door to a whole set of assumptions, among them simple, basic, rough, crude, rudimentary. The work at Morwenstow is none of these things. On the contrary, the stonecarving at Morwenstow is, if we look closely, so much more: a sophisticated expression of some of the most advanced sculpture in the southwest during the 12th century, and likely to be connected to powerful patrons both religious and secular.

Notes

1. Robert A. Maxwell, 'Modern Origins of Romanesque Sculpture' in Conrad Rudolph (*ed.*), *A Companion to Medieval Art: Romanesque and Gothic in Northern Europe*, (Chichester, 2006), pp.334–56.
2. Simon Jenkins, *England's Thousand Best Churches*, (London, 1999), p.77.
3. Colin Rhodes, *Primitivism and Modern Art*, (London, 1994), pp.13, 9.
4. Edmund Harold Sedding, *Norman Architecture in Cornwall: A Handbook to Old Cornish Ecclesiastical Architecture, with Notes on Ancient Manor Houses*, (London, 1909), p.291.
5. For a general introduction to the material that remains in the county see Alex Woodcock, 'Reconsidering the Romanesque Sculpture of Cornwall', *Journal of the Royal Institution of Cornwall*, (2015), pp.7–22.
6. For introductions to Kilpeck, Alne and other sites in these two counties see Malcolm Thurlby, *The Herefordshire School of Romanesque Sculpture*, (Logaston, 1999) and Rita Wood, *Romanesque Yorkshire*, (York, 2012). For wider context see also George Zarnecki's *English Romanesque Sculpture 1066–1140*, (London, 1951) and *Later English Romanesque Sculpture 1140–1210*, (London, 1953).
7. In contrast to the Cornish examples the Romanesque fonts of Devon have attracted a considerable body of work. See, for example, Kate Clarke's series of nine articles: Kate M. Clarke, 'The Baptismal Fonts of Devon', *Transactions of the Devonshire Association*, (1913–22), I, (1913), 45, pp.314–29; II, (1914), 46, pp.428–36; III (1915), 47, pp.349–56; IV (1916); 48, pp.302–19; V (1918), 50, pp.583–87; VI (1919), 51, pp.211–21; VII, (1920), 52, pp.327–35; VIII, (1921), 53, pp.226–31; IX, (1922), 54, pp.216–23, as well as Christina Corser, *A Catalogue of Norman Fonts in Devon*, 5 vols, unpublished MPhil thesis (Exeter, 1983); Rita Wood, 'The Romanesque Font at St Marychurch, Torquay', *Proceedings of the Devon Archaeological Society*, (2004), 62, pp.79–98; Alex Woodcock, 'Honeysuckle and Red Sandstone: Some Characteristics of Romanesque Stonecarving in South Devon', *Transactions of the Devonshire Association*, (2009), 141, pp.77–92.
8. Ann Preston-Jones and Elizabeth Okasha, *Corpus of Anglo-Saxon Stone Sculpture Volume XI: Early Cornish Sculpture*, (Oxford, 2013), pp.219–23.
9. Apart from a mention in Françoise Henry and George Zarnecki, 'Romanesque Arches Decorated with Human and Animal Heads', *Journal of the British Archaeological Association*, (1957), 20, pp.1–34, the north Devon sites are largely absent from the literature. The best discussion remains that in Jeffrey K. West, 'Two Romanesque Stone Carvings' in R. A. Higham, J. P. Allan and S. R. Blaylock 'Excavations at Okehampton Castle, Devon; Part 2, the Bailey', *Devon Archaeological Society Proceedings*, (1982), 40, pp.79–82.
10. For an introduction to the variety of chevron forms in 12th century architecture see Rachel Moss, *Romanesque Chevron Ornament: The Language of British, Norman and Irish Sculpture in the Twelfth Century*, (Oxford, 2009), pp.3–4.
11. L. E. Elliott-Binns, *Medieval Cornwall*, (London, 1955), p.76.
12. Ron Baxter, 'Beakhead Ornament and the Corpus of Romanesque Sculpture' *Historic Churches*, (2004), 11, pp.8–10.
13. W.G. Hoskins, *Devon*, (London, 1954), pp.355, 474 and 519.
14. B.W. Oliver, 'Some Notes on Shebbear and Durpley Castle', *Transactions of the Devonshire Association*, (1948), 80, pp.159–66.
15. For an introduction to some of the problems see Alex Woodcock, *Of Sirens and Centaurs: Medieval Sculpture at Exeter Cathedral*, (Exeter, 2013), pp.19–22.
16. C.S. Drake, *The Romanesque Fonts of Northern Europe and Scandinavia*, (Woodbridge, 2001), pp.59–68.
17. Pevsner (2014), p.361.
18. Sedding, *Norman Architecture*, (1909), p.290.

Exeter Cathedral and church architecture in Cornwall in the early 14th century

John Allan

In 1850 G.E. Street summarised his contemporaries' views of the medieval churches of Cornwall:

> Almost everyone will tell you that they are large, coarse, granite-built, mis formed piles; long, low and of universally similar character. Their redeeming features… [are] their steeples and their woodwork; but even these last, although elaborately rich… [are] of a wearisome monotony. Nor … could one learn that anything earlier and better existed.[1]

Street searched out examples of churches in the Decorated ('Middle Pointed') style of the late 13th and early 14th centuries; 'the result,' he wrote, 'was far beyond my expectation'.[2] He might have added that the Cornish works of this period outshine contemporary achievements in the more numerous parish churches of Devon. Although later commentators, Pevsner among them, have been kinder to the medieval churches of Cornwall, they have often characterised them as modest, provincial, and charmingly set in the landscape – delightful but hardly in the vanguard of architectural development. These judgements, of course, arose from examination of the buildings that stand today. In assessing the overall picture of medieval architectural development in Cornwall we should bear in mind that the most important churches have all been destroyed; almost nothing stands of the county's three most ambitious churches: Launceston Priory, Glasney College and Bodmin Priory. New archaeological finds from their sites, notably architectural fragments, now provide fresh information about them.

For the modern observer it takes an effort of the imagination to appreciate that there was a moment in the early 14th century when not only the cathedrals of Bristol, Wells and Exeter but such smaller west-country places as Ottery St Mary and Sherborne were in some regards in the forefront of European architecture.[3] Some of the most innovative works are attributable to two major figures in early 14th-century English building history: Thomas Witney and William Joy.[4] In this chapter I would like to draw attention to a number of churches in Cornwall which show clear artistic links to the output of

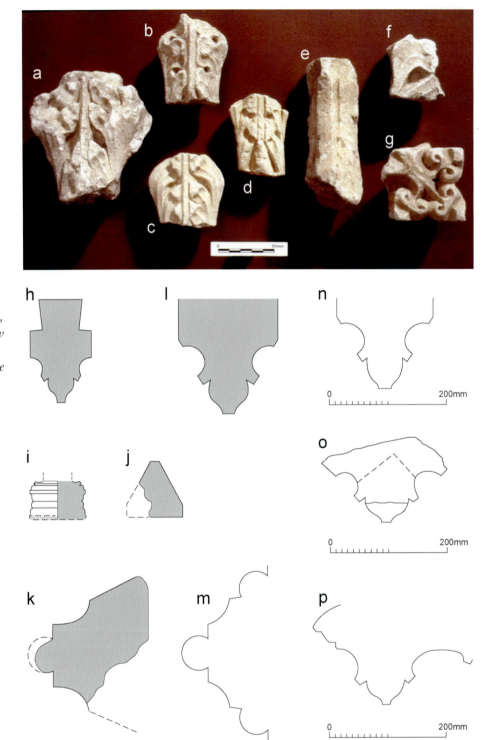

Fig. 1
(a–g) Beer stone architectural fragments from Glasney;
(h–k) Moulding profiles from Glasney: vault rib, shaft base, window mullion and pier;
(l, n) Profiles of the vault ribs of the Lady Chapel and choir, Ottery St Mary;
(m–p) mouldings from Exeter Cathedral's west front and Sherborne Abbey cloister
(photos: (a–g) G. Young; profiles (m–p) drawn by R. Morris, reproduced courtesy of the Dorset Archaeological and Natural History Society).

the workshop of Exeter Cathedral at the time that these two men were successively master mason there, showing that Cornwall participated in this exciting moment of architectural history.

I would like to start at Glasney College, Penryn, a foundation of Bishop Bronescombe of Exeter in 1265 and the object of much attention from his successors, notably Bishop Grandisson (1327–69).[5] As Nicholas Orme has recently emphasised,[6] Glasney was 'envisaged as being a smaller version of Exeter Cathedral'; it would be unsurprising therefore if its architecture, like its constitution, derived from the cathedral. The excavations conducted at Glasney by the Cornwall Archaeological Unit in 2003 recovered a large collection of stone fragments from the demolished church, allowing comparison to be made between some of its architectural details and those of other buildings.[7] A striking aspect of this collection is the extensive employment of Beer stone, a white chalk from south-east Devon. In the early 14th century this was not in widespread use, even in churches close to the quarries; it was particularly associated with the cathedral, where it became the most popular freestone after c. 1325, and with a number of closely related works such as the church of Ottery St Mary and monuments at Bere Ferrers.[8] At Glasney this exotic material was used on a large scale; it was employed for moulded structural stonework (for example in the vault and piers) and was apparently the sole material chosen for internal fittings. The latter include finials, crockets and other components from elaborate canopies of high quality whose fleshy bulbous foliage carvings are closely related to work at Exeter Cathedral (Fig.1a–g). They include pieces with rippling surfaces whose style is comparable to that introduced into the cathedral choir after c.1302 (Fig. 1a, 1c), sometimes called 'seaweed'; there is also at least one fragment (Fig.1g) with square leaves whose lower edges scroll back towards the central stem – a feature seen on the 'A' and 'B' registers (the lower and central tiers) of the cathedral's image screen of the 1340s.[9] Since work of this material and quality is rarely seen elsewhere in Cornwall and Devon, these furnishings were probably made by masons in the Exeter Cathedral workshop.

The structural fragments likewise suggest strong connections to Exeter and to closely related buildings, notably the college at Ottery St Mary, established by Bishop Grandisson in 1338. The tall moulded shaft bases, bell capitals and a window mullion with plain flat chamfers (Fig.1i–j) all find their parallels at Exeter. A more specific link may be drawn out in the case of the vaulting ribs. Five fragments from Glasney share the same moulding profile, in which the central fillet is flanked by ogee mouldings and deep hollows, with an outer pair of diagonally-set side fillets (Fig.1h). This rib form differs from the profiles used at Exeter in the period c. 1280–1340 but, as Richard Morris showed, it is found in the Lady Chapel vaults at Ottery St Mary,[10] and closely related variations of it occur in the west front image screen of Exeter Cathedral, in Bristol Cathedral and in the cloister vaults at Sherborne Abbey (Fig.1m–p).[11] A further link here is the use of this moulding in the high vault over the choir at Ottery – an important detail recorded by John Hayward in 1842 (Fig.1l).[12] All these works are in Beer stone. The image screen of the cathedral can firmly be attributed to the master mason William Joy; its mouldings are quite different from those of his predecessor at Exeter, Thomas Witney.[13] With this in mind, we may also note the similarity of the pier mouldings from Glasney to Joy's mouldings in the image screen (Fig.1m). Again the match of stylistic detail and of building stone amounts to good evidence that the vault, and possibly the piers, represented by the Glasney fragments were drawn in the Exeter workshop to designs by William Joy, probably in the period 1342–9.[14] Joy's vaults at Ottery, Wells and Bristol were in the forefront of European design; the recovery of bosses or other more diagnostic details may one day throw light on the intriguing question of the form of the Glasney vault.

The county's second major building project of the early 14th century about which exciting new evidence is now emerging was the rebuilding of the eastern limb of Launceston Priory. The ambitious scale of this programme is evident from a comparison of the eastern ends of the major churches of the diocese (Fig.2a), and is captured in Richard Parker's recent reconstruction drawing (Fig.2b). Some of the features of this work can be seen in the large and highly informative collection of architectural fragments from the site, many of them recently re-excavated from undergrowth by the Cornwall Archaeological Unit[15] and now the subject of an initial assessment by the writer (Fig.3a–b).[16] They show some general points of similarity to early 14th-century work at Exeter Cathedral. The most interesting is the evidence for elaborate late Decorated window tracery including flamboyant designs; so many different motifs are represented among the fragments that it seems likely that the priory, in common with the cathedral, displayed different window patterns in each bay. Unlike the finds at Glasney, however, the forms of the mouldings seem almost entirely different from those at Exeter (Fig.3c, f, h–l). The two vaulting rib profiles represented at the priory show similarities to work in the Bristol; the rather thick and heavy form (Rib 1: Fig.3f) is close to Morris' Type 1 at St Augustine's, Bristol (now Bristol Cathedral) (Fig.3g), whilst the central element of the more complex form of vault rib at Launceston (Rib 2: Fig.3c) recurs in mullion profiles at St Mary Redcliffe, Bristol and Berkeley Castle (Fig.3d–e) – but also at Ottery St Mary.[17] These quite different profiles probably represent two stages of work by different master masons; the late Richard Morris has proposed that his Bristol Cathedral Type 1 may be attributable to the master mason Nicholas de Derneford, whilst the works at Berkeley Castle, Mary Redcliffe and Ottery can be attributed with greater confidence to master William Joy.[18] We may suggest that the canons of Launceston looked to Bristol for their master mason on at least one occasion. This must have seemed their natural choice: St Augustine's was the most important house of the Austin canons in the region.[19] The Launceston choir had some unusual features; the elevations had continuous walls between the arcade piers rather than the free-standing piers which are almost universal elsewhere.

Two forms of furnishing at Launceston do however relate to Exeter. First, the priory had at least one elaborate pavement of heraldic tiles of c.1300 whose designs match those known from various ecclesiastical sites in Devon including Newenham Abbey, Axminster, and the church of the Greyfriars and the Bishop's Palace in Exeter.[20] As petrological study has shown,[21] these tiles were probably made near Exeter. Second, a screen rose at the back of the high altar. Only the rubble core of the altar survives above ground today (Fig.4a),[22] but removal of shrubbery from this area by the Cornwall Archaeological Unit showed that the altar front was formerly clad in Beer stone, a plain

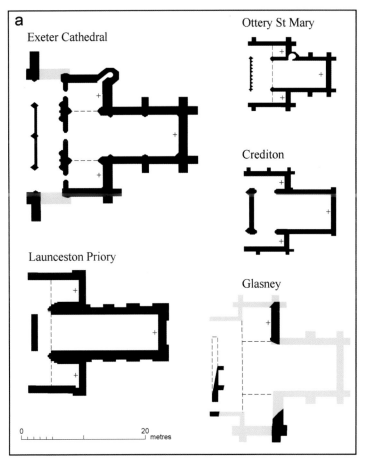

Fig. 2
(a) Comparative plans of the eastern ends of major churches in the diocese of Exeter. The large size of Launceston will be apparent;
(b) Launceston Priory: reconstruction drawing by Richard Parker, 2007.

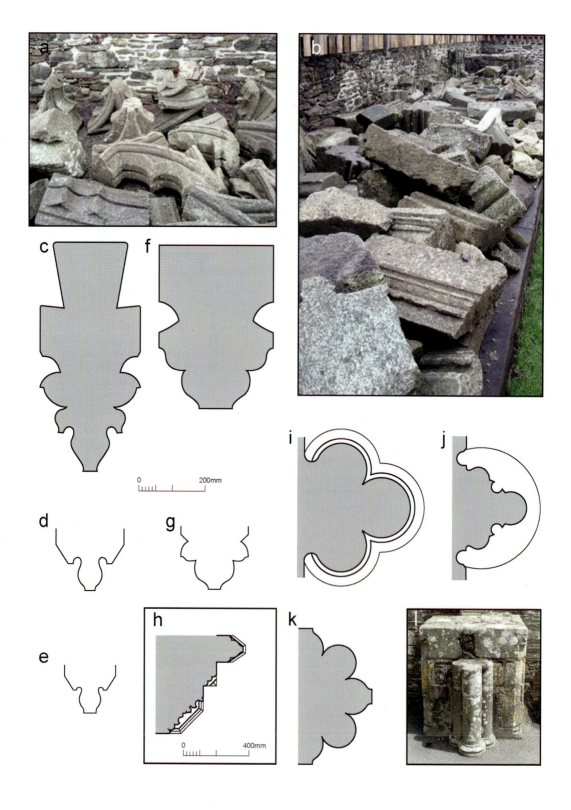

panel of which lay detached below its front face. A group of astonishingly delicate architectural fragments, also of Beer stone, was recovered from around the high altar by Arthur Wills in 1976 (Fig.4b–e). They include miniature shafts, finials and foliage carvings. One informative piece comes from a small ribbed vault, with the bottom of a small canopy rising from its front face and a boss of swirling foliage on the underside (Fig.4c–e). This is interpretable as part of a canopy over a seat or niche, perhaps comparable to the sedilia in the presbytery at Exeter or to a niche like those in the chancel at St Ive (discussed below). The find shows that Launceston was one of the group of major churches in south-west England which had elaborate screens at the back of the high altar. The two grand examples surviving today at Christchurch (Dorset) and Ottery St Mary (Devon)[23] are both works of the 1340s; both are believed to derive from the lost screen at Exeter built for Bishop Stapledon c.1316–24, which was the subject of lavish expenditure (Fig.9f-g).[24] These three furnishings hold an important place in the development of the late medieval reredos. Arthur Wills' finds show that the Launceston screen was comparable in quality to the sole surviving component of the Exeter high altar furnishing: the sedilia on its southern side. The fragment of hanging vault also suggests an interest in complex three-dimensional space which characterizes the Exeter composition.

Outside Launceston and Glasney, the main group of 14th-century churches relevant to our theme lies in south-east Cornwall: St Ive, Sheviock, South Hill, Tywardreath and the south-eastern chapel of St Germans. Their connections were first described by G.E. Street and are explored further by Peter Beacham in the new Pevsner.[25] The first four were initially cruciform parish churches;[26] at St Germans a magnificent chapel was added to the Norman church. These works are closely related to one another and have a number of unusual features in common (although not in every case): sedilia in the chancel;[27] doorways and other openings with segmental arches; broad chamfered plinths to the exterior below boldly projecting buttresses with prominent chamfered weatherings; extravagantly wide and richly moulded ogival tomb recesses with sub-cusping; and the use of Beer stone, albeit in varying amounts (Fig.6). A further connection is to be seen in their window tracery (Fig.5). Among a range of late Decorated patterns including reticulated ones, there are two distinctive motifs, both worked with slight variations at each church: a central circle with internal cusping, and a pair of ogival motifs similar to mouchettes, used at the head of the window lights (Figs5b–c, respectively (x) and (y)). The latter link us to the last stages of the Decorated work at Exeter Cathedral, where they occur in the west window (c.1328–42).

The lofty and richly decorated chapel added to the eastern end of the nave of St Germans Priory is an especially impressive member of the group; the new Pevsner rightly describes its 'high aesthetic qualities' and 'finesse of detail'.[28] The composition in its eastern wall, with a pair of tall windows separated by an elaborate central niche, all below a high central gable and window, marks it out as a superior structure. The chapel's decoration is especially well represented in the superb but mutilated sedile in the south wall, with its knobbly foliage, densely crocketed finials, diagonally-set shafts with sunken panels, sub-cusping, and bell capitals with abaci of multiple undercut mouldings – all features closely related to cathedral work of the 1320s to 1340s (some

Fig. 3 *Launceston Priory. (a–b) General views of the moulded stonework. (c) Vault rib. (d–e) Mullions at Berkeley Castle and St Mary Redcliffe, Bristol. (f–g) Vault ribs at Launceston and Bristol Cathedral. (h-l) Other Launceston mouldings (d, e & g reproduced from Morris 1997, Figs 1 & 2, by courtesy of the British Archaeological Association).*

56

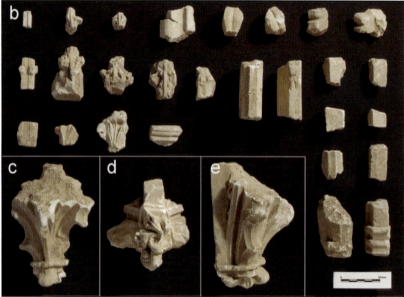

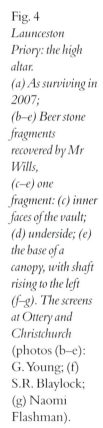

Fig. 4
Launceston Priory: the high altar.
(a) As surviving in 2007;
(b–e) Beer stone fragments recovered by Mr Wills,
(c–e) one fragment: (c) inner faces of the vault;
(d) underside; (e) the base of a canopy, with shaft rising to the left
(f–g). The screens at Ottery and Christchurch
(photos (b–e): G. Young; (f) S.R. Blaylock; (g) Naomi Flashman).

of them late in that period; the shafts with their sunken panels are close to those in the west front).

Of the group of parish churches, St Ive has the richest ornament and deserves particular attention. The chancel is especially rewarding. So fine are its carvings that, had the building been destroyed but a mere handful of these survived, we would know that the church was something out of the ordinary in Cornish medieval architecture. The east window, mainly in Beer stone, is a notable survival; it has perhaps the most inventive Decorated tracery design now surviving in Cornwall, and is in much better condition than most 14th-century windows in this building stone (Fig.5b). Other chancel features underline St Ive's connection to Exeter (Fig.6a, c–d, f–j). The pair of niches which flank the central window are again in Beer stone. Their nodding ogee heads display the same bell capitals and knobbly foliage as at St Germans (Fig.6d, i–j) and link once more to the cathedral; we may for example compare their crocketed shafts and large ball-like central finials with details in the cathedral's pulpitum (1318–26) and Bishop Stapeldon's tomb (after 1328) (Fig.6e–f).

No figure sculpture survives *in situ* in any of these churches, but three fragments of drapery at St Ive, again in Beer stone, and now loose in the church, present a further link to the cathedral; they seem to come from quite a large figure – perhaps too large to be from the niches flanking the high altar (Fig.7d). In the 1330s a new style of late Decorated figure sculpture emerged at Exeter, exemplified by the groups of sculpture in the south porch (Fig.7a) and the tiers of angels and kings (the 'A' and 'B' registers) of the image screen of its west front, which were undertaken in the following decade.[29] In its most developed form the style is characterised by restless figures in dramatic poses wearing richly decorated garments; a distinctive feature is the character of the draperies, in which the hem of the garment turns back and forth as the cloth hangs in broadening tubular folds. It has long been known that this style of sculpture is also to be seen in the rood screen at Christchurch, Dorset,[30] and in the pair of tombs to Otto and Beatrice Grandisson in the nave at Ottery St Mary, but the presence of Beer stone tomb sculptures in the same style in other parish churches in Devon seems to have escaped notice. They include the monuments to two members of the Beaupel family at Landkey and the effigy of a woman at Arlington, both in North Devon (Fig.7b–c). The style is also to be seen over the Somerset border at Combe Florey.[31] No Cornish monument in this style has been recognised so far, but the St Ive fragments show that it was formerly to be seen in the county.

Street wrote of this group of churches: 'there are so many marks of similarity in these examples that I venture to class them as the work of the same man.'[32] This seems a reasonable conclusion, although we may prefer to think of a team of masons rather than one individual. They worked in a mixture of local stone and the Beer stone popular at the cathedral, reserving the latter for the most delicate work. They were evidently well informed about developments in the Exeter workshop, and capable of highly skilled work.

Finally, high-quality early 14th-century fabric in two further Cornish churches may be discussed briefly: that at St Michael Penkevil and St Neot. The remarkably lavish treatment of the transeptal chapels at the former church, with sedilia, a piscina and other features in each transept, is similar in character to that seen in the group of churches discussed above, and once more some of this work at least is in Beer stone. Here too the tracery of one window has motifs in common with the west window of Exeter Cathedral (Fig.5k). Exactly how much of the fabric we now see is actually of early 14th-century date, however, needs much more careful re-examination.[33]

The point of interest at St Neot is the recess below a large ogee arch in the north chancel wall, which as Jo Mattingly has suggested may be the surviving part of the shrine of St Neot. Once again this is in Beer stone. The treatment of the foliage with broad fleshy plant motifs is different from that discussed so far, but one detail is reminiscent of Exeter and Ottery: the conceit of a broad foliage band in which the leaves alternate with shields whose suspension loops are threaded through the branches of the trees. This motif appears on the Grandisson tombs at Ottery St Mary – but also further afield.

It is a striking fact that almost all the works discussed in this chapter are datable on stylistic grounds to the second quarter of the 14th century. Documentary evidence for South Hill and St Ive supports this conclusion; their high altars were dedicated in 1333 and 1338 respectively.[34] The five churches in south-east Cornwall are so similar to one another that they all probably belong in the same decade, although some parallels to features in the chapel at St Germans may take us into the 1340s.[35] All four parish churches in the group seem to have been completely new structures. The provision of four new churches within a few years of one another in a specific part of the county looks more like a co-ordinated effort than a series of unrelated developments. Was this something that Bishop Grandisson himself might have initiated? It is well known that he was dissatisfied with (sometimes appalled by) the state of the church in Cornwall and was energetic in undertaking reforms.[36] Was it alternatively the result of a group of related local initiatives, perhaps by a mix of secular and clerical patrons? A significant figure here may have been Bartholomew de Castro, rector of St Ive from 1314 until c.1349, who was a senior figure in the church life of Cornwall, engaged for example in the administration of ecclesiastical courts, and a man with known links to Exeter;[37] he was once described by Charles Henderson as 'a right-hand man of Bishop Grandisson'.[38] Another may have been the rector of South Hill, John de Ferrers, who dedicated the high altar there in 1333; in the same year William Ferrers[39] set up an archpresbytery at Bere Ferrers, Devon, which like the Cornish works discussed here shows close links to the cathedral.

In the South Devon volume of the *Buildings of England* (1952), Pevsner commented that '…given its [Exeter Cathedral's] impressive scale and richness of architectural conception, it is extremely surprising that, with the exception of Ottery St Mary and a few windows here and there, it has virtually no influence on the diocese, i.e. either Devon or Cornwall.'[40] In the revised *Buildings of England* volumes for Devon and Cornwall, Bridget Cherry and Peter Beacham have drawn out more fully the connections between the cathedral and other churches.[41] In this chapter I have attempted to show that this process can be taken further. I have emphasised the point that the cathedral seems a much more isolated achievement in the diocese nowadays than it would have appeared in the Middle Ages; the greater churches – those mid-way between the mag-

Fig. 5
Window tracery.
(a) Exeter Cathedral, west window;
(b–d) St Ive;
(e–g) Sheviock;
(h) South Hill;
(i) St Germans;
(j) Tywardreath;
(k–l) St Michael Penkevil.

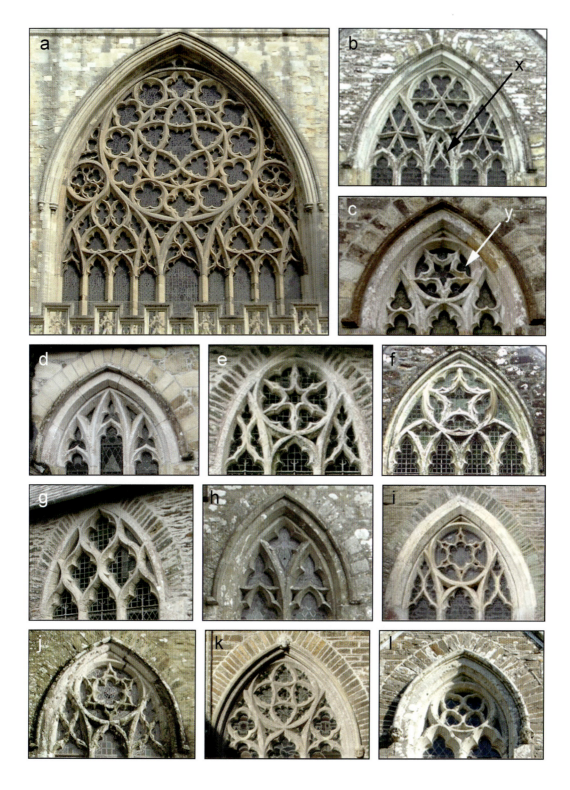

Fig. 6
Internal details. (a–b) Tomb niches at St Ive and South Hill; (c, f–g) Details of the sedilia at St Ive; (e) sedile at St Germans; (d, h) niche flanking east window, St Ive, with (i–j) finial and shaft of the tomb of Bishop Stapledon in Exeter Cathedral.

nificence of the cathedral and the much more limited resources of the parish church – have largely been destroyed. The discoveries at Glasney and Launceston Priory illustrate the ways in which archaeological investigation and the study of architectural fragments can go some way to bridging the gap between the two extremes. In both cases clear links to the cathedral emerge; we may imagine that similar connections might be found if equivalent evidence were available at the wealthier monastic houses of the diocese such as Plympton and Tavistock. Nevertheless, the cathedral was not the only source of masons and designs for major church building in early 14th-century Cornwall; the canons of Launceston evidently looked elsewhere for the master mason of the rebuilding of their Lady Chapel and choir. Other works in the county in the Decorated style, including some major ones such as Fowey and Lostwithiel (the latter regarded by Street as 'the pre-eminent church of Cornwall'),[42] show no obvious links to the cathedral.

Much remains to be pursued in this field. First, the results of the excavations con-

Fig. 7 *Exeter-style sculptures with tubular-folded draperies. (a) Exeter Cathedral south porch: the Annunciation; (b) Landkey; (c) Arlington; (d) St Ive* (photo (a): S.R. Blaylock).

ducted since the 1980s at the major sites of Glasney College, Bodmin Priory and Launceston Priory should be published. Second, we need detailed ('archaeological') building recording at many of the sites discussed here. In many instances there are for example uncertainties about the extent of 19th-century restoration of window tracery which could be resolved by careful inspection of stones and mortars, accompanied by measured drawing, geological analysis and related study of archival evidence. In this regard, progress with the church of St Michael Penkevil would be especially rewarding; at present it is difficult to determine how much of its medieval fabric is *in situ*; analysis may also resolve the question of whether the transepts are in part 13th-century work. A fuller measured record of mouldings at all these sites would be of great value. In Devon and Cornwall we also need a fresh systematic study of the tomb sculpture of the sort currently being pursued by the Gittos in Somerset. Despite these limitations, it seems clear that in the early 14th century a number of works of the highest quality were created in Cornwall, and the majority are attributable to the workshop with Exeter Cathedral and associated with its two most famous master masons, Thomas Witney and William Joy.

Acknowledgements

I am grateful to the following friends who have shared ideas and visited the churches discussed here with me: Peter Beacham, Stuart Blaylock, Jon Cannon, Jo Cox, Moira and Brian Gittos, Jo Mattingly, Nicholas Orme, Richard Parker and John Schofield. I am especially indebted to Stuart Blaylock, who has collaborated with me at Exeter and Glasney over many years and has kindly allowed me to use his photographs and line drawings.

Notes

1. Published three years later as G.E. Street, 'On the distinctive features of the Middle Pointed Churches of Cornwall', *Transactions of the Exeter Diocesan Architectural Society* (1853), ser.1, vol.4, pp.86–102.
2. *Ibid*. p.87.
3. The literature on the subject is extensive; of particular note however are papers contained in J. Cannon and B. Williamson, *The Medieval Art, Architecture and History of Bristol Cathedral: An Enigma Explored*, (Woodbridge, 2011). For a general overview see C. Wilson, *The Gothic Cathedral*, (London, 1990), pp.180–204.
4. John Harvey, *English Medieval Architects: a Biographical Dictionary down to 1550* (revised edition), (Gloucester, 1987), pp.338–41. R. Morris, 'Thomas of Witney in Exeter, Winchester and Wells' in F. Kelly (ed.), *Medieval Art and Architecture at Exeter Cathedral*, British Archaeological Association Conference Transactions for 1985, (1991), pp.57–84.
5. N. Orme, *A History of the County of Cornwall Volume II: Religious History to 1560*, (London, 2010), pp.255–6.
6. N. Orme, *Cornwall and the Cross: Christianity 500–1560*, (Chichester, 2007), p.246.
7. D. Cole, *Glasney College, Penryn, Cornwall*, Cornwall Archaeological Unit Report 2002R004 (2005). The collection was the subject of an initial assessment in J.P. Allan and S.R. Blaylock, *Archaeological Assessment of the Collection of Architectural Fragments, Ridge Tile and Pottery from Glasney College, Penryn, Cornwall*, in 2004, Exeter Archaeology Report 04.55. (2004). A full excavation report was to follow but has not been undertaken so far.
8. J.P. Allan, 'The building stones of the cathedral' in F. Kelly (ed.), *op.cite*, pp.10–18.
9. This form of foliage carving does however continue into the 15th century, so the fragment might be of later date.
10. R. Morris, L. Monckton and J. West, 'The worked stones and medieval architecture' in L. Keen and P. Ellis (eds.), *Sherborne Abbey and School: Excavations 1972–76 and 1990*, Dorset Archaeological Natural History Society Monograph 16, (2005), pp.92–7.
11. For Sherborne Abbey refer to *Ibid*, p.93, Fig.86. 4–5. For Exeter see R. Morris, *Witney*, p.68 and 78. For Bristol & Berkeley see R. Morris, 'European prodigy or regional eccentric? The rebuilding of St Augustine's Abbey Church, Bristol' in L. Keen (ed.), *Almost the Richest City, Medieval Art and Architecture at Exeter Cathedral*, British Archaeological Association Conference Transactions, XIX, (1997), pp.41–56.
12. J. Hayward, [Drawings and architectural description in] F.G. Coleridge and J. Hayward, 'An account of the church of

Ottery St Mary', *Transactions of the Exeter Diocesan Architectural Society* (1842) ser.1, vol.1, pp.3–63.
13 R. Morris, *Witney*, p.68, 78. J.P. Allan and S.R. Blaylock, 'The Structural History of the West Front' in F. Kelly (ed.), *op.cite*, pp.98–103.
14 For Exeter see R. Morris, *Witney*, p.68 and 78. For Sherborne Abbey refer to R. Morris *et al*, 'The worked stones and medieval architecture', p.93, Fig.86. 4–5. For reservations that every work in this style can necessarily be attributed to the master see *ibid.*, pp.92–7.
15 J. Gossip, *St Thomas' Priory, Launceston, Cornwall*, Cornwall Archaeological Unit Report, 2002R004, (2002).
16 J.P. Allan, *Notes towards an Architectural History of Launceston Priory*, Exeter Archaeology Report, 09.58 (2009). More work is needed on this matter; I am collecting material for a fuller study.
17 Hayward, *op.cite*, Plate 5, window jamb in Lady Chapel.
18 Morris, *European prodigy*, pp.43–50. Interpretation of the sequence remains controversial: see Morris' replies to both C. Wilson, 'Gothic metamorphosed: the Choir of St Augustine's Abbey in Bristol and the renewal of European architecture around 1300' in Cannon and Williamson (eds.), *op.cite*, pp.69–147 and P. Crossley, 'Bristol Cathedral and Nikolaus Pevsner: *Sondergotik*' in *Ibid*, pp.184–215.
19 As Nicholas Orme has pointed out to me.
20 Tiles in Lawrence House Museum, Launceston include examples with the arms of Richard of Cornwall. For the corresponding tiles at Exeter Greyfriars see J.P.Allan and L.Keen, 'The medieval floor-tiles' in J.P. Allan, *Medieval and Post-Medieval Finds from Exeter, 1971–1980*, Exeter Archaeological Report. 3 (1984), pp.232–47; for Newenham refer to J.P. Allan and R.J. Silvester, 'Newenham Abbey, Axminster', *Proceedings of the Devon Archaeological Society* 39, (1981), pp.159–71. For the Bishop's Palace, Exeter, see descriptions in Devon Heritage Centre Z19/15/11 and Z19/15/18 [Pulman correspondence with Pitman Jones, 1846].
21 R.T. Taylor, 'Petrological study of floor-tiles from Launceston Priory' in Allan (ed.), *Launceston Priory*, pp.9–11 and subsequent examination of related tiles.
22 The vertical trenches in the rubble presumably represent the robbed positions of freestone – perhaps the bases of shafts rising behind the altar.
23 The front heavily restored but the rear intact: B. Cherry and N. Pevsner, *The Buildings of England. Devon*, revised edition, (London, 1989), pp.619–20.
24 See two articles by V. Sekules, 'The liturgical furnishings of the choir of Exeter Cathedral' in Kelly (ed.), *op. cite*. pp.172–9 and 'Early 14th-century liturgical furnishings' in M. Swanton (ed.), *Exeter Cathedral: a Celebration*, (Exeter, 1991) pp.111–15 also C. Tracy with A. Budge, *Britain's Medieval Episcopal Thrones: History, Archaeology and Conservation*, (Oxford, 2015). For the relationship of the Christchurch reredos to Exeter see P. Williamson, 'Sculptures of the West Front' in Swanton (ed.), *op.cite*, pp.78–80.
25 Street, *op.cite*, pp.91–4; Pevsner (2014), pp.27–8 and individual church entries.
26 This is no longer apparent at Tywardreath, which was rebuilt in 1880–7; these remarks follow Street's description and interpretation prior to that work (Street, *op.cite*, p.93).
27 Street, *op.cite*, p.94 pointed out that these are 'almost the only examples in the county'. Beacham notes, however, that the sedilia at South Hill may be of earlier date (Pevsner (2014), p.619.
28 Pevsner (2014), p.545.
29 The addition of the image screen was underway by 1346–7; the fact that sculpture in this style was not provided for every niche, and the work was completed with simpler sculptures attributable to the late 14th century, suggests that the composition was incomplete at the time of the Black Death in 1348/9: Allan and Blaylock, *West Front* in Kelly (ed.), *op.cite.*, pp.98–102.
30 A. Gardner, *English Medieval Sculpture*, (Cambridge, 1951), p.222.
31 B. Gittos and M. Gittos, 'Motivation and choice: the selection of medieval secular effigies' in P. Coss and M. Keen (eds), *Heraldry, Pageantry and Social Display in Medieval England* (Woodbridge,2002), pp.143–67. They have also discussed other figures in this style in Ham Hill stone in B. Gittos and M. Gittos, 'Medieval Ham Hill stone monuments in context', *Journal of British Archaeological Association*, 165, (2012), pp. 89–121. Related monuments in Berkshire, Wiltshire and Somerset are discussed by R. Emmerson, 'The fourteenth-century tomb effigies at Aldworth, Berkshire, and their relationship to the figures on the west screen of Exeter Cathedral' in S. Badham and S. Oosterwijk (eds), *Monumental Industry: The Production of Tomb Monuments in England and Wales in the Long Fourteenth Century* (Donington, 2010), pp.97–113.
32 Street, *op.cite*, p.93.
33 I am inclined to regard the transepts as early 14th-century additions relating to the college of chantry priests set up by Sir John Treiague in 1320 (for which see Orme, *History*, pp. 226–8) but Beacham in Pevsner (2014) p.587 suggests that the features of the south transept fit well the church dedication date of 1261. In support of a later date it may be noted that they are of Beer stone – a material in widespread use only after c.1320/25.
34 F.C. Hingeston-Randolph, *The Register of John de Grandisson, Bishop of Exeter, Part I* (London, 1894), *Part II* (London, 1897): 1331–1360; *Part III* (Exeter, 1899): 1360–1369, *Part II*, p.718, 758.
35 Orme, *History*, p.187 and Pevsner (2014), pp.544–5 are surely right in dating the chapel to 'about the 1330s' and 'c. 1330' rather than the 1360s, as earlier commentators had proposed.
36 Hingeston-Randolph, Part 3, pp.i-xxxviii; Orme, *Cornwall and the Cross*, p.67 and 72 and *History*, p.49, 52 and *passim*.

37 *Ibid*, p.62; see also, Part I, p.409, 530; 1897, 682, 727, 758, 837 and 900.
38 C. Henderson, *Cornish Church Guide and Parochial History of Cornwall*, (London, 1925), p.84.
39 Hingeston-Randolph, *op.cite*, Part II, p.718.
40 N. Pevsner, *The Buildings of England: South Devon*, (Harmondsworth, 1952), p.139.
41 Cherry and Pevsner, *op.cite*; Pevsner (2014).
42 Street, *op.cite*, p.88.

'The Longest, Strongest and Fairest that the Shire Could Muster – Wade-Bridge'[1]

Andrew Langdon

Wade-Bridge is situated on the river Camel in north Cornwall, 5½ miles south-east of the river estuary at Padstow. Scheduled as an ancient monument in 1928 and now grade 2★ listed, the bridge links the parishes of St Breock on the western bank with Egloshayle on the eastern side and also the ancient hundreds of Pydar and Trigg. Since its medieval foundation the bridge has changed significantly: once seventeen arches long, today it stands four arches shorter and three and a half times wider. This chapter will consider the past, present and future of this bridge, a structure described by previous generations as 'magnificent', 'noble' and 'the most celebrated in the county' and portrayed in various editions of *Cornwall* as 'one of the best medieval bridges in England'.[2]

Before the bridge was built, there was a small hamlet or village on the western bank of the river known as Wade, Old English wæd, 'a ford'.[3] Once the bridge was built it became known as Wade-Bridge, or 'the bridge at Wade'; the present town of Wadebridge did not develop until the early-18th century. Most publications record only one date for construction; however such a large bridge would have taken many years to build.[4] Indeed, delays would have been inevitable: building would have been seasonal as lime mortar cannot be used in cold winter weather and being built on a tidal river the foundations of the piers could only have been constructed at low tide.

John Lovibond, a vicar of Egloshayle, is credited with being the mastermind behind the building of Wade-Bridge.[5] In the Ministers' Accounts for 1461–2, it is recorded that he received a license to draw stone from a quarry within the manor of Penmayne in St Minver Lowlands, this appears the most likely date for the start of construction.[6] In 1476, Lovibond set up a Bridge Trust that was endowed with land and property in Egloshayle which was subsequently leased out to provide an income for maintaining the bridge. As this would have been done when it was completed or near completion a suggestion that it took fifteen years to build is reasonable.[7] In 1478 William of Worcester makes reference to the bridge, although according to his itinerary he did not visit it personally. If nothing else this suggests that its existence was an important talking point throughout Cornwall at the time.[8]

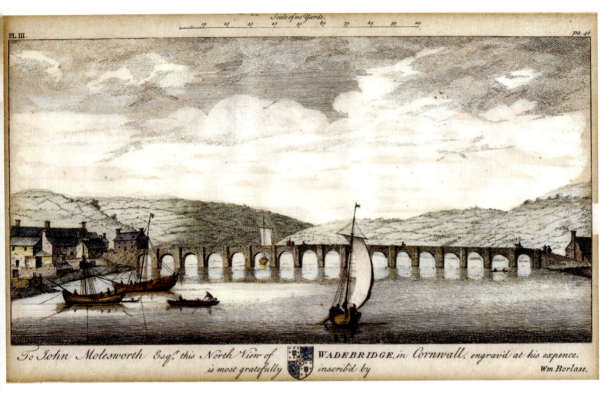

Fig. 1
Illustration from The Natural History of Cornwall, (1758) by William Borlase.
Mr Andrew Eddy.

The bridge was built at the highest point which large vessels could reach and almost the lowest place where the river could be easily forded,[9] and was built between two medieval chapels, St Michael's on the St Breock bank of the river and the King's chapel on the Egloshayle side. Neither chapel survives today. References to St Michael's chapel exist in the St Breock churchwardens accounts[10] and both are recorded as being sold in the Calendar of Patent Rolls in 1591.[11]

The legend of the 'Bridge on Wool', recorded by John Leland in 1538 about sixty years after the bridge was completed, tells how Lovibond struggled to find firm footings for some of the piers because of quick-sand and used packs of sheeps' wool for a foundation.[12] Similar accounts have been recorded for Bideford Bridge, London Bridge and St Ives Bridge in Cambridgeshire; however Wade-Bridge's claim is the earliest.[13] Unfortunately no evidence supports the claim so while it may have been true perhaps it remains a 'play on words' or a metaphor to suggest the bridge was built from the profits of the wool trade.

What is certain is that the medieval engineers would have found the conditions challenging. Finding bedrock on the west or St Breock side of the river is difficult as was discovered by the engineers who did test bores of the river bed in April 1956.[14] They found that on the south-west (St Breock) side they had to drill down 17.4m (57 feet) to find bedrock while on the Egloshayle side (known as Bridge End) bedrock was closer to the surface. The obvious conclusion of this is that the bridge was most likely constructed from the Egloshayle side towards the St Breock bank, as the builders could

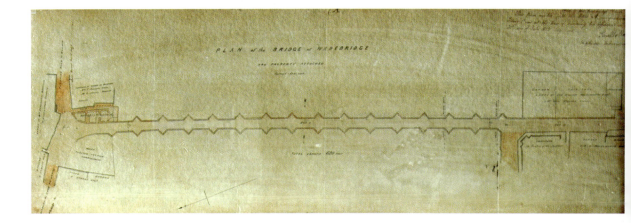

Fig. 2
Plan of bridge in 1852, prior to the first widening scheme.
Wadebridge Town Council.

start with firm abutments in the rock and build out into the river.[15] Nevertheless, Lovibond somehow overcame the problem with foundations, as the bridge was built of seventeen uniform arches: the fact that each arch is uniform width means that every pier was set down exactly in the correct position and not necessarily where bedrock could be found. So regardless of the legend, secure but shallow foundations were created.

Another mystery is how the medieval builders set the foundations. Two common methods were either to drive wooden piles into the river bed, which could then have been infilled with barge loads of stone to form a platform to set the piers of the bridge on, or the creation of primitive coffer dams which could be deployed at low tide. During the 20th century engineers have investigated the foundations on numerous occasions, but no reports exist to indicate what the piers were sitting on.

No plans, illustrations, or paintings of the bridge survive from the 15th or 16th centuries. However good indications of what the bridge looked like can be seen on a late-17th century painting on a frieze in the parlour room at Trevelver Farm in St Minver Highlands, while a much larger 18th century painting of the bridge hangs in Pencarrow House at Washaway, near Bodmin. From the 18th century an illustration by William Borlase of 1758 (Fig.1) remains one of the best examples. It was not until 1852 when the bridge was to be widened for the first time that a detailed plan of the structure was created. This plan was drawn by Henry Coom, who signed an affidavit confirming that it was an accurate representation of Wade-Bridge and its approaches (Fig.2). With its causeway, the structure was 270.3m (680 feet) long and 3m (10 feet) wide, the actual seventeen arch bridge measuring 153.3m (503 feet) when complete. With its walled causeway and long narrow roadway the bridge was originally an extremely impressive building.

Surviving documents from the Bridge Trust show that leasing Trust land and property provided an income which helped towards the maintenance of the bridge, likewise tolls or pontage paid to pass over the bridge provided further revenue.[16] The trustees for Wade-Bridge employed a Bridge Warden to oversee the general maintenance of the bridge and each November held an annual meeting where the warden would account

Fig. 3
Watercolour drawing showing the proposed widening of the central arches of the bridge in 1818.
Wadebridge Town Council.

for his expenditure throughout the preceding year.

One of the major concerns for visiting ships was the silting up of the river which meant that they could only reach Wade-Bridge on a spring or very high tide. Records suggest that by c.1800 the quaysides had been extended into the river to narrow the flow of the channels and create a greater depth of water on the ebb tide, causing the first and the last arches to be stopped up. On the upstream, Egloshayle, side of the river was Bridge House, which was built up against the first arch, thereby creating a cellar to the property. This arch still exists today, as a locked cellar, and in the back can be seen a blocked doorway which once led into the basement of Bridge House.

For the first three hundred years the bridge was wide enough to carry all the traffic of the day, which consisted mainly of pedestrians, mounted horses, hand-carts and animals travelling to market – there would have been little wheeled transport as the roads were so bad. Even though the bridge existed, it seemed that many travellers preferred to travel down the north coast, through Delabole, St Endellion and across the river estuary by ferry from Rock to Padstow.[17] However this changed in 1760 when the new turnpike road from Hallworthy to Mitchell was created, which brought greater volumes of wheeled traffic over Wade-Bridge.

In 1818 a plan was put forward to widen the roadway of the three central arches of the bridge, so that coaches and carriages could pass on the middle of the bridge. In the town hall at Wadebridge hangs a watercolour showing a bridge with an ornate central parapet and what appear to be lamps above (Fig.3).[18] This proposal to widen the bridge never came to fruition. In July 1845 however Wombwell's travelling circus and menagerie, which consisted of many long horse-drawn wagons of caged animals, had considerable difficulty crossing the bridge and as a consequence seriously damaged the parapets on both the up and downstream sides.[19] To alleviate continual damage spar stones were set against the parapets at either end of the bridge to try and restrict the width of vehicles crossing – an idea which is still in use on several medieval bridges today.

Between the 14 and 26 July 1845 a traffic census, commissioned by the County Sessions, showed that in thirteen days, 372 carriages, 1,207 carts, 1,398 horses, 280 cattle and 21,848 pedestrians crossed the bridge.[20] In 1847, an agreement was reached between the Wade-Bridge Trust and the County Sessions that the Trust would be wound-up and their assets passed over to the County in order to facilitate a widening scheme. An announcement was made in local newspapers for architects and builders to submit tenders to widen the bridge on both sides.[21] Plans were submitted to widen the bridge in either stone or with cast-iron parapets; the council opted for the cast iron as this would allow for an additional foot in width to be achieved.[22]

However, on Thursday 8 July 1847 a great flood on the rivers Camel and Inny completely destroyed or badly damaged all bridges in its wake except Helland Bridge and Wade-Bridge.[23] Such was the disaster that the widening of Wade-Bridge was postponed

Fig. 4
The second widening of the bridge in 1963. Miss May Garland

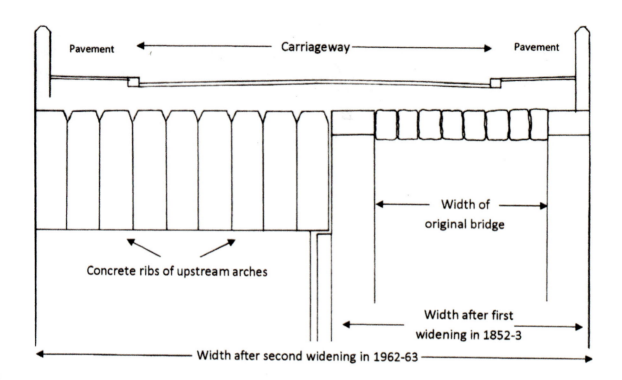

in order to rebuild or repair the resulting damage and nothing was done at Wade-Bridge until 1852 when the Trust was wound-up and Bridge House was demolished to allow for widening by three feet on either side. By this time the idea of an iron parapet had been dropped in flavour of stone. To enable widening new segmental arches were extended out over the existing cutwaters supported by blocks of moorland granite. The County Sessions reported that by October 1852 five arches had been widened on one side, that figure rising to nine by January 1853 despite the builders being held up by incessant heavy rain.[24] In October 1853, it was reported at the Cornwall Michaelmas Sessions that the widening had been completed.[25] Charles Henderson, Cornish historian and author of *Old Cornish Bridges and Streams*, later criticized the method used stating that 'the new arches diminish the depth of the cutwaters upon which the beauty of the old bridge largely depended'.[26]

By 1868, arches sixteen and fifteen were dry as the quaysides on the town (or St Breock) side of the bridge were further extended into the river. At this time, John Martyn caused some controversy by erecting a warehouse on the edge of the new quay thereby blocking both arches.[27] Despite being built with permission from the County Bridge Surveyor, Silvanus William Jenkin, the County Sessions commissioned the civil engineer James Henderson to carry out a structural survey to ascertain if blocking these additional arches would have any negative affect on the bridge. Henderson's report stated that blocking the arches did not prejudice the bridge however he did consider that any further encroachment on the waterway would create greater scouring of the pier bases and so should be avoided.

There was always much disagreement between the various owners of the quays on both sides of the river. Training walls were built in the river to divert the flow of the ebb tide so that some quays had a much greater depth of water than the others. In 1878, a more drastic proposal was made by owners on the Egloshayle bank to extend their quays outwards all the way up to the bridge, so causing the second, third and fourth arches to be blocked up. This time Henderson's advice was taken and the proposed encroachment and issue of the training walls was taken up by the Board of Trade, which refused permission for any more arches to be blocked and insisted that the training walls should be realigned so as to give an equal flow of water to the quaysides on both sides of the river.[28]

With the introduction of motor vehicles early in the 20th century, there was again a need to widen the bridge. Concerns were voiced about the dangers to school children walking across the bridge with no pavements and the many accidents on its narrow approaches.[29] In 1957, the Royal Fine Art Commission provided three possible proposals to relieve the traffic problems; the first, to build a new bridge downstream, the second to widen the existing bridge with cantilevering as at Bideford and finally, to widen the bridge while attempting to keep the existing character. The latter option was agreed, to widen the bridge from 4.8m (16 feet) to 11m (36 feet) on the upstream side of the bridge in a similar style to the original structure.[30]

Work started in March 1962, when a temporary pedestrian footbridge was set up along the downstream side of the bridge, while the upstream island and river banks were raised to accommodate workshops and a construction site. Reinforced concrete

Fig. 5
Opposite, above
Cross-section showing the original bridge sandwiched between the two widening schemes. Author.

Fig. 6
Opposite, below
Bridge as seen from downstream on a high tide. Author.

piles were driven (13.7m) 45 feet into the riverbed to support the new piers of the bridge, which grew from the western end of the bridge towards Egloshayle (Fig.4). New concrete arch ribs were cast on the upstream island. Despite very cold weather, work progressed well with the new part of the bridge being finished enough to take all the Royal Cornwall Show traffic in June 1963.[31] The newly-widened bridge was finally completed in August of that year.[32] At last pedestrians could walk across the bridge on wide pavements safe from the traffic, in particular children walking to school. However, historian A. L. Rowse criticized the widening, stating that they had 'destroyed something irreplaceable'.[33]

A cross section of the bridge shows the original medieval bridge sandwiched between the 19th century widening and the 1960s widening on the left hand side (Fig.5). However, by the early 1970s a crack had appeared down the centre of the road and although repaired by Council workmen it kept reappearing. This was eventually found to be the result of a slight movement between the original bridge and the modern 1960s structure, the latter built on reinforced concrete piles was rigid, with no movement; whereas the original bridge had only shallow foundations which flexed with the motion of the riverbed. The result was a shift of 5cms, and a gap where water started to percolate down through, causing spalling of the reinforced concrete arches.[34]

In 1975, contractors reinforced the foundations and strengthened the old bridge so that there was no movement between old and new.[35] This involved piling around the old piers of the bridge with high tensile steel bars, which were then tied into horizontal bars set into the bottoms of the piers. All were concreted over to form starlings around each pier. This will have completely ruined any future possibility of an archaeological investigation into the foundations of the original bridge. Finally, the walls and piers of the old bridge had deep holes drilled into them and tons of liquid grout pumped in under pressure. Nevertheless, further corrosion of the reinforcing steel has taken place, leading to concrete breaking away and exposing rusting metal. In 1987, extensive repairs were made to the arch ribs by Cornwall County Council workmen. Large areas of concrete were cut back, the steelwork treated and the concrete renewed.[36] During 2009, further work took place to consolidate these arches.[37]

In conclusion, the concern for the bridge in the 21st century will be more related to the 1960s upstream section than the medieval or 19th century parts of the structure. Indeed, as the concrete arch ribs continue to corrode, further repairs are likely to be required. Although Wade-Bridge has been shortened and widened and filled with grout, the core of the bridge is still medieval. Whether it is still the strongest and fairest is open to question, but it certainly remains the longest medieval bridge in the county, at 128.6m (422 feet) with thirteen open arches (Fig.6).

Notes

1. F. E. Halliday (ed.), *Richard Carew, A Survey of Cornwall*, 1602, (London, 1969), p.219. Andrew G. Langdon, *Wade-Bridge: Notes on the history of the fifteenth century bridge*, (St Agnes, 2012).
2. Fortescue Hitchins, *The History of Cornwall*, (Helston, 1842), pp.525–7. Pevsner (1951), pp.216–7; Pevsner (1970), p.238; Pevsner (2014), p.691.
3. O. J. Padel, *A Popular Dictionary of Cornish Place-Names*, (Penzance, 1988), p.176.
4. William Hals, *The Compleat History of Cornwal: General and Parochial*, (Truro, 1750), p.111; John Maclean, *The Parochial and Family History of the Deanery of Trigg Minor*, (Bodmin, 1879), III, p.17; Joseph Polsue, *A Complete Parochial History of the County of Cornwall*, (Truro, 1867), I, p.128.
5. Maclean, *Ibid*, p.17.
6. NA SC6/821/11, Ministers' Accounts (1461–2, 1 & 2 Edward IV).
7. CRO DDX.450/181.
8. John H. Harvey, *William of Worcester Itineraries* (Oxford, 1969), pp.16, 17, 30, 31, 90 and 91.
9. James West, *St Breock and Wadebridge: A contribution to a History of Parish and Town*, (Redruth, 1991), p.31.
10. CRO DDP19/5/1.
11. NA C66/1382 m24, Calendar of Patent Rolls, 1591, 34 Elizabeth. Part 4, m24.
12. Polsue, op.cite, IV, Supplementary notes, p.69.
13. W. G. Fearnside and T. Harrel, *London Bridge*, (London, 1838), p.64; J. Westwood, *Albion: A Guide to Legendary Britain*, (London, 1985), p.217; F. E. Whiting, *The Long Bridge of Bideford – through the centuries*, (with additions by P. Christie), (Bideford, 1997), p.21 and Bob Burn-Murdoch, *St Ives Bridge and Chapel*, (St Ives, 2001), p.12.
14. *Western Morning News*, Friday 4 May 1956.
15. Langdon, *op.cite*, p.22.
16. CRO DDX450/100 to DDX450/184, also documents in the Courtney Library, Royal Institution of Cornwall.
17. John Ogilby's strip map of 1675 shows the main road from St Endellion leading down to Rock and across the estuary to Padstow, rather than going to Egloshayle and across the river over Wade-Bridge.
18. CRO DDX450/180/1 and DDX450/180/2.
19. *West Briton & Cornwall Advertiser*, 17 October 1845.
20. *Idem*.
21. *West Briton & Cornwall Advertiser*, 16 July 1847.
22. *Cornwall Royal Gazette*, 8 January 1847, Report on the Cornwall Epiphany Sessions.
23. *West Briton & Cornwall Advertiser*, Friday 16 July 1847; *Royal Cornwall Gazette*, Friday 16 July 1847.
24. *Royal Cornwall Gazette*, 22 October 1852.
25. *Royal Cornwall Gazette*, 21 October 1853; *West Briton & Cornwall Advertiser*, 21 October 1853.
26. Charles Henderson and Henry Coates, *Old Cornish Bridges and Streams* (Truro, 1972) p.119.
27. *West Briton & Cornwall Advertiser*, 7 January 1869, 'The alleged encroachments at Wadebridge'.
28. CRO AU3/8/5/54.
29. *Western Morning News*, 3 October 1956, '17 accidents on or at approaches to bridge'.
30. *Western Morning News*, 31 December 1957, 'Royal Fine Art Commission: Proposed widening, complete reconstruction of bridge'.
31. The Royal Cornwall Agricultural Show moved to a permanent site on the west side of Wadebridge in 1960, and the old bridge was a major bottleneck which could not be avoided for people travelling to the show from east Cornwall.
32. *Cornish Guardian*, 22 August 1963, 'Bridge widening scheme complete'.
33. A.L. Rowse, *The Cornishman Abroad*, (London, 1976), p.232.
34. R. L. C. Stephens and J. L. Carlyon, 'The history, repair and upkeep of a highway structure Scheduled as an Ancient Monument', *Proceedings of the Institute of Civil Engineers*, 103, (September, 1994), pp.157–162.
35. *Cornish Guardian*, 18 September 1975.
36. *Pers. Comm.* John Armstrong, Bridge Department, Cornwall Council, 9 June 2011.
37. *Pers. Comm.* Mark Hollow, *Area Structures Maintenance Technician*, Cornwall Council, 9 October 2014.

If only Pevsner had started in the Midlands: making sense of Cornwall's Perpendicular church architecture

Joanna Mattingly

Of the pre-Victorian churches in Cornwall, Peter Beacham concludes that 'the vast majority date predominantly from the Perpendicular period'.[1] Although this phenomenon of English architectural history prevailed from the middle of the 14th century, in Cornwall it first appeared in the 1460s with the rebuilding of St Petroc's church in Bodmin. Yet, rather than being a period of architectural innovation for the county it proved to be an age of standardisation, a time when the ideal church was of three-hall construction with parallel gabled ranges of equal or similar width and landscape-dominating towers. Documentary sources and dendrochronology dating show that church enlargement in Cornwall continued through the Reformation leaving the majority of Cornish churches unfinished as aisles became redundant.[2] The revised first edition of Pevsner provides a springboard for re-dating.[3] This chapter will focus on major Cornish churches, most of which achieved three-hall form, during three key periods – first, between 1450 and 1485, a period of civil turmoil during the Wars of the Roses; second, during the early part of the 1500s and lastly, during the Reformation period between the 1520s and 1570s.

The early- to mid-15th century was a period of great experimentation. At least twelve different pier types have been identified in medieval Cornish churches, and almost all were still in use or coming into use during this period. They include square or round piers with four attached shafts, octagonal piers, prototype Cornish standard piers with pronounced hollow chamfers and fillets as seen at St Cleer and St Martin by Looe. Moreover, Cornish standard piers with four attached shafts with hollow chamfers are evident in the south chapel at Liskeard (1430) while more elaborate versions with limestone (or sand-rock) wave mouldings appear at St Just in Penwith and St Ives between 1410 and 1434.[4] At Stratton in 1348 we first see square piers with four attached shafts, these continue into the 15th century, examples being St Stephen, Launceston (1419), St Columb Major (1433), Sennen (1441) and Callington (c.1458). Octagonal piers enjoyed an even longer life spanning from c.1236, as seen at Crantock, to 1595 and later at Paul where a cheap rebuilding was necessitated by the Spanish Raid.[5]

Along with trialling different kinds of architectural detail, church widening was a major concern for the late medieval church. Dateable crenelated lean-to south aisles are evident at St Germans, where the parochial aisle was widened and heightened between 1422 and 1455 during the episcopate of Bishop Edmund Lacy of Exeter. His coat of arms appears on a label of a large Perpendicular-style window separated from the next by a buttress (the westernmost window of this aisle, curiously, still has a Decorated or geometric feel about it). At Callington the crenelated south aisle with Perpendicular-style windows, square piers with attached shafts and a clerestory was described as 'newly edified' in 1466/7, probably dates from c.1458.[6]

The curious double north chapels at Gwinear and Constantine also appear to be of an early- to mid-15th century date, both being earlier than their respective south aisles.[7] Both places had significant saint's cults — a 14th century life survives for St Gwinear which features a stag, a carving of which appears on one of the octagonal pillar capitals in the outer or Arundell aisle (Fig.1). Wills confirm that a fraternity or guild of St Gwinear was active in the period between 1445 and 1470 and records show that new vestments were needed in 1462, the probable date of the outer chapel.[8] At Constantine, where the north aisle has square piers with attached shafts and the outermost or Bosahan aisle which has similar piers with triangular incision at the corner, the patron saint was a Cornish king.[9]

Fig. 1
In the north (Arundell) aisle at Gwinear a mid-15th century carving of a stag denotes the link with the cult of St Gwinear who had a vision whilst stag hunting in France. Author.

Callington's top-heavy Perpendicular style tower has set back buttresses to the second stage and pinnacles rising through the third stage supported on corbels depicting symbols of the Evangelists.[10] Dating from the 1440s it is a likely influence for similar features at Calstock, Lanlivery and St Austell in Cornwall.[11] At Launceston, St Mary Magdalene's detached tower existed by 1413 when collections were made for its bells.[12] It may well be a prototype for the Perpendicular set-back buttress type tower. St Mary Magdalene's church also has unique round piers with four triple attached shafts.[13] Were these recycled from an early to mid-15th century chapel that preceded the present church?

Early- to mid-15th century chapels at St Just in Penwith and Padstow include the same flamboyant-style windows and capitals with roses, foliage, acorns and identical four-petalled flowers.[14] The first of these churches has wave-moulded piers and Devon capitals with angels like St Ives and early Perpendicular reticulated south aisle windows with Jesus and Mary monograms on the labels of the hood moulds. Padstow, by contrast, has prototype Cornish standard piers with a wider than usual chamfer and narrow capitals; a type also found at Mawgan in Pydar and on the St Issey shrine.[15]

Padstow's south chapel was probably first built as a chantry chapel for Sir John Nanfan who made his will in 1446 but did not die until c.1459.[16] Clearly built in his life-time, this has some of the best mid-15th century external sculpture in Cornwall, though subjected to iconoclasm later. Nanfan's coat of arms appear on a shield held by a young boy in short tunic and hose with flowing hair, with royal beasts either side– probably the antelope and lion of Henry VI whom Nanfan served (Fig.2). At the east ends of this chapel, the chancel and the north aisle, there are elaborate inner arch decorations (Fig.3) found also at Cury and Sithney on the Lizard. This inner arch decoration is associated at Cury with a window type found later at Duloe with cusped tracery, the points of the cusps being enriched with cylindrical mouldings with fleurons which *Cornwall* dates to the late 14th to early 15th century, but is more likely to be mid-15th century.[17]

At St Ives, the south chapel (or Trenwith aisle) was probably added in the mid-15th century to a completed three-hall church.[18] With wave-moulded piers and Devon capitals, this chapel was the burial place, and probable chantry, of Otto Trenwith who died in 1462/3. An earlier drawing of Otto's now much defaced brass, shows him in heraldic tabard with flat cap and long gown, and external corbel heads exhibit Padstow hair-styling.[19]

Fig. 2
St Petroc, Padstow. The coat of arms of Sir John Nanfan appears on a mid-15th century crested shield held by a young boy situated above a buttress on the south chapel. Author.

Also dating from the Wars of the Roses period are towers at Fowey and Lanlivery. The former definitely, and the latter possibly, bearing the ragged staff badge of the Earl of Warwick who was executed in 1472. The earl owned the manor of Lantyan in both parishes and his tenant Laurence Kylwyth of Lanlivery was arrested and imprisoned by Henry Bodrugan esquire in the early 1460s around the time the tower was being built.[20] At Lanlivery (Fig.4), though not at Fowey, elements of the patron saint's life may have crept into the stonework, as at Gwinear.[21]

St Austell's Pentewan stone tower is commonly dated to between 1478 and 1487, however thanks to art historical work done by Pam Dodds it is now thought to be a decade or so earlier. The Courtenay coat of arms of three torteaux or discs with label, the cadency mark for an elder son, must refer to Edward Courtenay, son and heir of Hugh Courtenay. The Courtenays held the manor of Treverbyn Courtenay in St Austell parish and Hugh died at the battle of Tewkesbury in 1471.[22] The style of its external carving – sculptures of the Trinity,

Fig. 3
St Petroc's, Padstow. Detail of interior window arch of possible Nanfan chantry of mid-15th century date. Author.

Annunciation, Resurrected Christ flanked by St Mewan and St Austell, and twelve apostles – fits this revised 1460s dating. A pair of donor figures that flank the Resurrected Christ can be matched in brasses from the mid-1450s to early 1470s. The cropped male hair-style also features on the shrine at St Issey.[23]

Bodmin church is one of the best documented building projects anywhere in Britain, building accounts survive between 1469 and 1472, the latter date carved on oak wall plates in the south chapel though fitting out work including pulpit and pews went on into the 1490s.[24] In a three-year campaign starting in 1469 Richard Richowe and other masons built the walls of the south chapel and south aisle and constructed Cornish standard Perpendicular piers and windows beginning in the north chapel where earlier Perpendicular-style tracery can be seen. Another major church, Liskeard, has a south chapel with similar Cornish standard piers which date from the 1430s.[25]

The Bodmin accounts suggest that different carpenters worked on different roofs as at St Veep c.1460.[26] John Sam was paid over £30 for the north and south aisle roofs leaving William Carpenter of Bideford to work on the nave or middle roof.[27] Faced in Pentewan, Bodmin's crenelations are fanciful 19th century restorations and originally the church was like St Andrew's in Plymouth, built between 1460 and 1488, and probably by the same architect.

A Perpendicular chantry chapel with Cornish standard granite piers and capitals of more easily carved granite was also added to St Winnow church at this time.[28] William Kayle of Ethy and his wife Phillipa nee Trenoweth appear in this chapel's east window as donors and their marriage contract of 1463 survives. It seems that William died soon after and Philippa went on to marry John Carminow.[29]

The chantry chapel on the north side of Duloe church is a Perpendicular jewel and was built during his life by the childless Sir John Colshull.[30] The chapel is crenelated,

Fig. 4 *Detail of external carving at Lanlivery church c.1460s showing what look like a pair of severed heads.* Pam Dodds.

has animal corbels like the Trenwith chapel at St Ives, three-light windows like Bodmin's north chapel, a north east window like Cury, an inverted green man and a defaced tomb that once stood under the most easterly arch where Colshull could stare, in death (1483), into the eyes of a soul-transporting angel.

Moving on to the early-16th century, two completed projects that demonstrate exemplary granite ashlar work are the south aisles of St Neot and North Hill (Fig.5) with crenelations and pinnacles.[31] Peter Beacham suggests the same architect for these and Liskeard's slate and granite outer south aisle. St Neot's south chapel and aisle can be dated to the 1480s and first decade of the 16th century while Liskeard's is clearly a decade or two later than its north aisle dated between 1477 and 1480. A similar contrast of materials with stylistic similarities can be seen at St Mary's Truro, St Mary Magdalene's Launceston and Probus.[32] The south aisle of the first, executed in a local elvan stone, was clearly the model for the second and third. The parish church in Truro began in 1504 with the granting of a quarry licence and concluded in 1518 with glazing. John Holton, son of a Bodmin mason, was probably mason here with his father and on his own later at Camborne.[33] St Mary Magdalene's extraordinary granite exterior, by contrast, spans a period from 1511 to 1544. Begun by 1523, Probus's Somerset-style tower had Tregian patrons as did Truro.

Building accounts of similar quality and detail to the Bodmin church accounts sur-

Fig. 5
St Torney, North Hill 1500s south aisle, described by Nikolaus Pevsner as 'A large and specially ambitiously decorated church' and, in the recent edition of Cornwall as 'One of Cornwall's most enjoyable churches'. Author.

vive for North Petherwin (1505–7 and 1518–24) and the Berry chapel in Bodmin (1501–14).[34] Both show a significant change mid-project from the softer granites of the St Austell area or Hingston Down to much coarser Bodmin Moor granite. At North Petherwin whiter granite gives way to browner Bodmin Moor granite. Masons were paid at Hingston Down near Cotehele on Valentine's Day 1507, but later in the same year took a licence for a quarry at Rowtor on Bodmin Moor. At Berry chapel the mason Harry Sleman drew stones for the lower south window of the tower from a St Austell area quarry in 1508, but in 1509/10 brought in moor stone, identifiable as Bodmin Moor granite, for the four upper windows. Thus in the 1500s, for the first time, granite was available in considerable quantities at a, presumably, much cheaper price than before. This coincided or perhaps contributed to granite becoming the material of first choice, at least for internal piers.

The final period under consideration here, the Reformation, was a time of catch-up when many smaller churches tried (but mostly failed) to achieve the three-hall plan. One of the churches that succeeded was Camborne where Devon style capitals and South Hams windows point to a date of enlargement from the 1520s to 1540s. Churchwardens' accounts confirm that a northern Lady Chapel was begun in 1538 by John Hotton and therefore must have been finished in the mid-to late-1540s.[35]

Even in the case of large and impressive churches like Fowey which never lost their

Fig. 6
The panelled porch at St Sidinus at Sithney, similar in style to other churches around the Roseland and Lizard areas, all with a suggested early 16th century date. Author.

clerestory or early 14th century octagonal piers or suffered a reduction in height, building work continued into the 1530s and 1540s. The highly carved nave ceiling with Tudor angels has now been dated by dendrochronology to this time, with lean-to roofs in the south aisle being of 1500s date – a rare example of a non-three-hall church.[36] This Reformation date for the nave roof relates to the introduction of a rood screen and loft. Wooden screens painted to look like stone now marked the divide between chancel and nave, making chancel arches redundant all over Cornwall.

Panelled porches, of which there are over a dozen Cornish examples and counting, may also belong to this period rather than earlier (Fig.6). Most retain their waggon roofs so could be dated by dendrochronology. Clearly a west Cornwall fashion, though Mylor has stylistic links with the early 16th century porch doorway at St Austell, most were worked in granite, sometimes with accompanying buttresses. Arches are four-centred, round headed, or, as at Gunwalloe, of basket form, with blank-trefoil headed tracery carving on the responds. Only one domestic example is known at Godolphin in Breage parish, where the church has a similar porch entrance.[37] Three to five bands of tracery are normal, sometimes topped and tailed with trefoils, and parallels can be found on tower pinnacles and between the upper windows of Prior Vivian's porch at Rialton in St Columb Minor which must date between 1508 and 1533.

Some post Reformation Perpendicular projects still remain to be identified, unlike Devon.[38] A dated south aisle at Morwenstow of 1564 certainly has South Hams style-windows and Cornish standard piers. The lateness here can be explained by the fact that Morwenstow is about as far from granite as any parish in Cornwall and its tower was unfinished in 1548. At Calstock the northern mortuary chapel of the Edgcumbe family dates from 1588, possibly replacing an earlier chapel. Cornwall St Teath's tower (1630) and Falmouth's parish church exterior (1662–70s) can certainly be considered as among the latest expressions of Perpendicular Gothic architecture.

Forged in a melting pot of ideas in the first half of the 15th century, Cornish Perpendicular architecture may not, after all, be so far removed in time from the starting date assigned to it elsewhere (c.1377 at Exeter Cathedral), but it endured far longer. Dating most Cornish Perpendicular architecture to the 15th century, as Nikolaus Pevsner did back in 1951, is clearly no longer tenable. Further dendrochronology dating studies are eagerly awaited to elucidate this fascinating period of architectural, and sculptural, achievement against the odds.[39]

Notes

1. Pevsner (2014), p. 28. Unless otherwise specified dates are from the corrected 2014 version.
2. Joanna Mattingly, *Looking at Cornish Churches*, (Redruth, 2005). Perpendicular aisles had to be wide in order to house side altars and processions.
3. The revised edition was published in 2014. This volume carried corrections by, amongst others, this author.
4. Pevsner (2014), p.29, shows sections of the two most common pier types.
5. Joanna Mattingly, *Cornwall and the Coast: Mousehole and Newlyn*, (Chichester, 2008), pp.20, 36–7. Smaller churches and chapels like St Levan and Zennor adopted this type of Perpendicular arcade.
6. Nicholas Orme (ed.), *Cornish Wills 1342–1540*, (Exeter 2007), p.85.
7. Pevsner, (2014), p.156 misdates Constantine's south aisle to c.1420 and the sequence should be reversed.
8. Nicholas Orme, *The Saints of Cornwall*, (Oxford 2000), p.136–8. Orme, *Cornish Wills*, pp.74, pp.204–5.
9. Orme, *Saints*, pp.94–6.
10. St Luke's winged bull appears on the corbel nearest the porch and is the least worn.
11. Bridget Cherry and Nikolaus Pevsner, *Devon*, (London, 1989), p.868.
12. Richard Peter and Otto Peter, *The Histories of Launceston and Dunheved*, (Plymouth, 1885), p.116.
13. Pevsner (2014), plate 67.
14. Most probably the work of the same masons. A chapel at Colebrooke in Devon with flamboyant window is dated c.1460 by Cherry and Pevsner, *op cite*, p.276.
15. Pevsner (2014), plate 31.
16. Orme, *Cornish Wills*, p.75, 235. In 1446 Nanfan left money to found a chantry at Tewkesbury.
17. Pevsner (2014), p.171. The place from which the Nanfans took their name is in Cury parish.
18. *Ibid*, plates 35 and 46.
19. William Lack, H. Martin Stuchfield and Philip Whittemore, *The Monumental Brasses of Cornwall*, (London 1997), pp.120–1.
20. Ragged staffs appear over the west window at Fowey and as a mullion to a round stair window high up on the tower at Lanlivery. Peter Beacham and John Allan remain unconvinced by the latter. For Lantyan refer to NA C1/28/338. This was part of a power struggle within Yorkist ranks.
21. Orme, *Cornish Wills*, p.76 suggests Lanlivery's saint Brivet may mean 'short life' and a tower corbel shows angels

holding what may be her head with a giant's head below. Could St Brivet have been a virgin saint and, like St Agnes, beset by the unwanted attentions of a giant? For St Agnes see H.L. Douch and P.A.S. Pool (eds.), 'The Parish of St Agnes by Thomas Tonkin', *Journal of the Royal Institution of Cornwall* (1975/6), pp.197–210.

22. Pevsner, (2014), p.496 mistakenly says the arms are of Peter Courtenay who was bishop of Exeter between 1478 and 1487, hence the incorrect dating.
23. Lack *et al*, *op.cite*, p.181 for Fowey and Quethiock.
24. CRO, B/Bod 244 and J.J. Wilkinson, 'The receipts and expenses in the building of Bodmin Church', *Camden Society* vii, new ser. 14, (1875), pp.1–49. Pevsner (2014), plate 68.
25. P.L. Hull (ed.), *The Cartulary of Launceston Priory*, (Torquay 1987), pp.186–7 (no.507).
26. Information on St Veep from Eric Berry and N.W. Alcock (ed.), 'Tree-Ring Date Lists 2006', *Vernacular Architecture*, Vol.37, Issue 1, (2006), p.111. Were older piers retained twice here in c.1460 and c.1540 when existing aisles were widened and re-roofed?
27. Wilkinson, *op.cite*, pp.19,-20, 28–9, 31.
28. Pevsner (2014), plate 14.
29. Library of Royal Institution of Cornwall HA/3/3. I am grateful to Angela Broome for drawing my attention to this. The eldest Carminow daughter was a donor of the St Kew Passion window c.1490. See Michael Swift, 'Anglican Stained Glass in Cornwall and its Social Context', *Journal of the Royal Institution of Cornwall* (2009) ,p.18, plate 5 image of William Kayle, not Archdekne as stated there.
30. Pevsner (2014), plate 49.
31. *Ibid*, plate 34.
32. *Ibid*, plate 63 and 64.
33. NA C1/568/87; CRO, PD322/1.
34. CRO, B/Bod 314/1; P167/5/1. Surprisingly no reference is made to either set of accounts in Cornwall or Devon.
35. Pevsner (2014), p.137 dates Camborne's south aisle to the 15th century but an early 16th century date seems more likely.
36. Pevsner (2014), plate 30.
37. Pevsner (2014) dates Breage's panelled porch to c.1460 and, by implication, that at Constantine to c.1420. The other church examples are Budock, St Erth, Gorran, Gunwalloe, St Just-in-Roseland, Lelant, Mullion, Mylor, Ruan Major and Sithney.
38. Howard Colvin, 'Church Building in Devon in the Sixteenth Century', *Essays in English Architectural History*, (New Haven and London ,1999), pp.22–51.
39. Cherry and Pevsner, *op.cite*, pp.42–3.

'Ghastly Good Taste': the Cornish Country House 1540–1840

Paul Holden

Our conference title – 'Only a Cornishman would have the endurance to carve intractable granite' – derives from a John Betjeman phrase that, although far from the truth, does highlight the exertion and strain needed to sculpt the county's indigenous building stone.[1] It was, in part, the inflexibility of native materials that inclined Pevsner to open his 1951 guide with the words 'Cornwall possesses little of the highest aesthetic quality though much that is lovable and much that is moving'.[2] This chapter draws on this, perhaps the most provocative opening sentence from any of the Pevsner county guides. It will consider whether the Cornish house is actually lacking in aesthetic quality or rather should be seen as enigmatic, a product of the unusual relationship that Cornwall has had in the past with incoming architectural tastes.

It is fair to say that many Cornish houses have developed piecemeal over time. Hence it was commonplace for country house owners to extend their property around a much earlier core, sometimes in a sympathetic provincial style but often adopting prevailing fashions in architectural design. This has, at times, created stylistic paradoxes which could aptly be called 'ghastly good taste' – another Betjemanesque expression used as the title of his book that takes an irreverent look at architecture and architectural history.[3] Examples might include Henry Harrison's Gothic porch and entrance hall (1829) on the west front of Port Eliot, a fine piece of architecture in its own right but which, some would argue, sits uncomfortably alongside the earlier building phases; William Wilkins' 19th century Tudor Gothic alterations at Tregothnan and Pentillie; George Wightwick's neo-Palladian east front at Pencarrow (1844–46) and, to go to extremes, Edwin Lutyens' 1920s strikingly modern extension on the side of the 17th century Penheale.

However true it may be to suggest that country houses suffered with fragmentary development, it is fair to point out that Cornwall did possess buildings of the highest aesthetic order, many of which are now sadly lost. Mount Edgcumbe (Fig. 1), prior to being struck by an enemy bomb during the Second World War, was a house of epic proportions and exquisite grandeur. It was the antithesis of the provincial medieval-style, low, inward-looking courtyard houses, of which Cornwall had many (perhaps the most

Fig. 1
Mount Edgcumbe. An exemplar of Tudor design principles which, along with Stowe House on the north coast of Cornwall, has to rate as one of the most historically cutting-edge architectural statements in the county.
© National Trust/ Lanhydrock

notable example remains Cotehele, the home of the Edgcumbe family from 1353). Situated on a prominent exposed slope high above Plymouth Sound, Mount Edgcumbe asserted itself with progressive styling that not only marked the arrival of the Renaissance into Cornwall but also provided physical proof that Cornish patrons aspired to buildings of first-rate quality. With its protected hall plan and towers at each corner, the enlightened design dates from 1547 and was arguably adapted from contemporary illustrations contained in Sebastiano Serlio's *Five Books of Architecture* (as indeed were earlier incarnations of the plan at Wollaton in Nottinghamshire and Longleat in Wiltshire, both by the prodigy house architect Robert Smythson). So fashionable was Mount Edgcumbe that King Charles II visited it twice in the 1670s, while several contemporary travellers regarded the house and its wider landscape as equivalent in beauty to Naples. To enhance the views from the house, the central hall was disproportionately heightened above the main body of the building and lit by clerestory windows.

Less grand, although in its own way as impressive, is Trerice, near Newquay (Fig.2). In the early 1570s the medieval manor house was extended using locally quarried silver-grey Elvan limestone. Gone was the outmoded medieval courtyard style design. In came a fashionable E-shaped plan, the centrepiece of which was a medieval-style, double-height Great Hall complete with good quality ornamental plasterwork. Despite the old medieval buildings breaking the rhythmic symmetry of the new frontage, the eye

Fig. 2
An 18th-century watercolour by George Sheppard showing the east front of Trerice.
©National Trust Images/John Hammond

overlooks such a discrepancy to focus on the striking Dutch gables, possibly the earliest examples of this feature in England. For a house which incorporates so many progressive features, it is a surprise not to see any classical orders applied to the façade, although to be fair to the unknown designers of Trerice, John Shute's book *The First and Chief Grounds of Architecture* and the first English translation of Serlio were still ten and twenty-eight years away respectively.

We cannot be so forgiving to a group of significant houses built between the last years of the Tudor dynasty and the middle years of the Stuart reigns. Prideaux Place, overlooking Padstow, set a precedent for a series of plain, mock-fortified, E-shaped gentry houses, later examples being Penheale near Launceston, Tregarden near St Mabyn, Pelyn near Lostwithiel and Trewan near St Columb. All share similar Tudor Gothic architectural forms, all follow similar plans and contain comparable details such as fireplaces and plasterwork; none however have a known architect or builder. Lanhydrock, near Bodmin, remains the most impressive of this canon (Fig.3). Yet it too breaks convention. The plan draws on earlier precedents with its unfashionable double courtyard arrangement while the building itself incorporates low and battlemented walls, heavy doorframes with carved spandrels and thick granite mullion windows. There were undoubtedly semblances of fashion. Inside, the house had an ingenious floor plan, using corridors to by-pass reception rooms for private access and, like many gentry seats of the period, it boasted more than one gallery (one on the north side and one along the now demolished east front). Furthermore, the plasterwork at Lanhydrock far exceeds the complexity and grandeur of any of the aforementioned houses.[4] A good example of how the Cornish adapted fashions can be seen on the Gatehouse. Completed in 1651 this granite mock-fortified structure has two distinctly different design principles applied to its front and rear elevations. The inner elevation (facing west) is of Gothic design with blind tracery, while the columns and arches of the east-facing outer elevation acknowledge elements of Renaissance design. Similar details can be seen at Trewan.[5]

Not all 17th century buildings display such sobriety. Ince Castle, near Saltash, with its red-brick French Renaissance-style façade suggests a pastoral acceptance of urban design. At first sight Ince appears very contemporary; however, on further investigation, it can be seen that the design is far from cutting-edge, having been inspired by Philibert de l'Orme's designs for a French chateau published some seventy years earlier.[6] Much further west, Godolphin touches on classical advances in its wonderful garden colonnade with paired rooms above, which Peter Beacham describes as 'astonishing' and 'a daring essay in Renaissance planning' (Fig.4).[7] 'Astonishing' it most certainly is, if only in finding such a feature so far west.[8] 'Daring' undoubtedly, again in the context of Cornwall, but Peter is rightly cautious in reserving judgement about its quality, which has a touch of the provincial builder about it. It is perhaps an example of 'ghastly good taste', whereby an idea which most likely took root in London (where Sir William Godolphin attended Court and Palladian architecture was the 'language' of its courtiers) suffered from both rudimentary execution and incompleteness because of the onset of the Civil War.

Undoubtedly the most daring exercise in Cornish Renaissance was Stowe near

Fig. 3
The Gatehouse with Lanhydrock House beyond.
©National Trust Images/John Millar

Fig. 4
Godolphin House, near Helston, the north front and colonnade. Once the home of Queen Anne's Lord High Treasurer, Sidney Godolphin.
©National Trust Images/Andrew Butler

Kilkhampton, aptly described by Tim Mowl as 'the wrong house and the wrong garden in the wrong place'.[9] Stowe was an exemplar of Franco-Dutch formalism, its use of red brick and Portland stone details (quite alien to granite country) were undoubtedly influenced by Clarendon House in Piccadilly which was built between 1664 and 1667 by Roger Pratt. So 'good' was Stowe that in 1698 Celia Fiennes regarded it as the finest house in England, while in 1736 the traveller John Loveday added that it was 'the finest seat in these western parts'; however, so 'ghastly' was its situation on the inhospitable north Cornish coast that by 1740 it had been demolished and its architectural salvage spread far and wide.[10]

By the turn of the 18th century architectural fashions had changed. The polite, understated Queen Anne movement left few major impacts on Cornwall: Croan near Wadebridge, Menabilly near Fowey, Trereife near Penzance and Trehane near Probus (lost to fire in 1946) being some of the most notable examples. But soon after the Hanoverian succession, two seminal manuals of Palladian taste were published – the *Vitruvius Britannicus, Or The British Architect*, by Colen Campbell and the first English translation of Palladio's *The Four Books of Architecture (I quattro libri dell'architettura)*. The main subscriber groups to *Vitruvius Britannicus* were members of the peerage, and tradesmen employed in physical building activity. Only two Cornish patrons subscribed, neither of whom were inspired enough to build.

The first faithful rendition of this new fashion in Cornwall was Antony House near Torpoint which despite its confidence, symmetry and double-piled elegance, remains modest when compared to houses illustrated in *Vitruvius Britannicus* (Fig.5). Many have

Fig. 5
The north front of the house at Antony.
©National Trust Images/Andrew Butler

tried to attribute the ancestral seat of the Carew family to James Gibbs, the most sought-after country house architect of the 1720s. As none of his buildings were illustrated in *Vitruvius Britannicus*, in 1728 Gibbs brought out his own *Book of Architecture* which includes an engraving of an untitled house in the south west, most likely Antony, showing the newly installed wings. Despite various attempts no one has been able to distinguish convincingly between the work of provincial builders such as Abel Croad and John Moyle (and others who may have emanated out of Devonport dockyard) and the more knowledgeable Gibbs whose hand is arguably evident at Antony, Bake and Trewithen.

Within a few years of Antony, true Italian classicism arrived at Pencarrow where a new piazza-style garden front was added in 1730 to the earlier north-facing T-shaped house. This radical frontage may well have been inspired by the Molesworths' Irish cousins as an almost identical façade was built at Castletown near Dublin slightly earlier by the native Italian architect Alessandro Galilei.[11] More restrained is Trewithen, near Probus, far more Gibbsian in style than Antony, perhaps explained by the fact that Phillip Hawkins subscribed to Gibbs's book but not to the publication of *Vitruvius Britannicus* or the English translation of Palladio. The house was much altered, firstly in the 1750s by Thomas Edwards of Greenwich and then again in the 1760s by Matthew Brettingham and Sir Robert Taylor who produced plans which, if fully executed, would have given us the most inspired and perfect example of ordered classicism in the county. Sadly, Trewithen's rebuilding was halted in 1766 when Thomas Hawkins (nephew of Phillip, from whom he inherited the estate in 1737 when he was only fourteen) died unexpectedly after having himself inoculated against smallpox as an example to his tenants. Had Hawkins lived, not only would Cornwall have its only surviving example of Chinoiserie interiors but a dramatic classical façade to match.[12]

Another subscriber to Gibbs's *Book of Architecture* was Thomas Edwards who built several Palladian-inspired houses for wealthy Cornish patrons. His style took the form of a simplified, provincial take on Palladian theory, drawing on printed precedents for inspiration. Tehidy, his first Cornish commission of 1735, for example, was an east-facing house with four detached pavilions, one at each angle, which consisted of a chapel complete with clock, a green-house and domestic offices. It was a design plucked straight from Palladio and dumped without ceremony into what one commentator referred to as a 'sad situation'. Tragically Edwards' patron, the mining magnate John Pendarves Basset, never got to see his house completed – he died of smallpox aged 25.

Two further designs heavily influenced by Palladio were Nanswhyden, near St Columb, and Carclew, near Truro. Nanswhyden was a curious structure, the purist in Edwards' canon, English Palladianism at its finest having no classical orders on display but typical Palladian features such as the rusticated base, dentiled pediment and the external double staircase. In some respects it was a reduced and much simplified version of Colen Campbell's Wanstead House, built a generation earlier. Edwards' patron for the new house at Carclew was the mining magnate William Lemon who, like Edwards, had subscribed to Isaac Ware's 1738 edition of Palladio. Built in granite and incorporating an Ionic portico with pavilion wings and a Doric colonnade, Carclew was undoubtedly the highpoint of Edwards' career, despite James Boswell's lukewarm appraisal after his visit there in 1792 when he wrote 'It is a substantial house, much improved by its present owner, the rooms are large and comfortable. There are a few good pictures'.[13]

Unfortunately all three of these houses – Tehidy, Nanswhyden and Carclew – succumbed to fire, though some remnants of each remain. Surviving to the rear of Carclew is a lovely example of stylistic diversity: a 'Gothick' single-chambered banqueting or summer house built in the prevailing style of Batty Langley but with a 'Gothick'/Rococo hybrid plasterwork ceiling.

Towards the end of the 18th century, architecture was perceived as scenery more than ever before. Two houses that stand out as exemplars of the Picturesque movement are Tregenna Castle of 1774 near St Ives and Acton Castle, built a year later, overlooking Mount's Bay. Both command sea views and are built in a clumpy Tudor 'Gothick' style. In his *Parochial History* Lake suggests that the architect of both was John Wood, a point much contested as to whether he meant the masterly John Wood the Younger of Bath or his younger contemporary William Wood (no relation) of Truro.

William Wood, a prolific local builder/architect, was ever ready to adapt a style and apply it to a building. He was not alone: other practitioners of the period included John Bland, John Eveleigh, Joseph Pascoe and Charles Rawlinson. Together their significant output and ability to adapt to various architectural styles has resulted in much confusion over the attribution of buildings. Rawlinson, a carpenter from Lostwithiel, for example worked in several styles at Boconnoc, Catchfrench, Clowance, Port Eliot and

Fig. 6
Saunders Hill, Padstow. House built for Thomas Rawlings by William Richards, who was most likely had associations with Sir John Soane's office. The house was demolished by 1824. Author.

Lanhydrock, where in 1784 he removed the east range of the mansion to reveal a more fashionable E-shaped house and most likely added a pair of 'Gothick' gate lodges on the northern edge of the estate.[14] Another, William Richards, seems to have merged elements of Sir John Soane's Tyringham Hall and Pitzhanger Manor into a design for Saunders Hill (Fig.6), a house once situated in what is now the carpark overlooking Padstow.

Throughout the 18th century and into the early 19th we begin to see more significant out-of-county architects crossing the Tamar: Robert Mylne and Lord Pembroke for example advising at Clowance, Sir Jeffry Wyatville at Trebartha and Sir John Soane at Port Eliot. Sadly it was Soane's huge argument with Humphry Repton at Port Eliot in 1804 that consigned the landscape gardener's proposed Gothic-style cloister connecting the house to St Germans' Priory to the scrap heap of 'ghastly good taste'. Another notable incomer was John Nash, architect of the Royal Brighton Pavilion, whose antiquarian picturesque Gothic-inspired castle at Caerhays is an exemplar of good taste, but with a ghastly twist. Of the asymmetrical castle with crenellated parapets, Sarah Gregor wrote

> Mr Trevanion replaced the old fashioned place of his ancestors by a most inappropriate castellated mansion, which being erected by Nash (who thought more of plan than of execution), was absurdly roofed with papier-mâché, a new invention of the day, which Mr Nash was certainly not justified in recommend-

ing to an inexperienced young man in a county so proverbially wet as Cornwall. The consequence was that when this roof, cracked by the sun and penetrated by wet, ceased to protect the interior, there was no means of mending it, and thus after assisting to choose the site, I lived to see the new house a desolate ruin for many years.[15]

We end with Trelissick, where in 1825 Thomas Daniell commissioned the architect Peter Frederick Robinson, a pupil of Henry Holland, to add a monumental six-columned Greek Doric portico in the style of an Athenian temple to the existing south front of his modest country house at Feock. The broad design was later published in Robinson's book *Designs for Ornamental Villas* (1827). It is an exemplar of transient good taste, only to become 'ghastly' by the reproving finger of the Victorians.

My aim in this chapter has been to explore aesthetic quality in the Cornish house and to place it in a wider context of architectural taste and fashion. It is fair to say while there are very good examples of country house architecture in Cornwall, the provincial twist on prevailing fashions has created some artless and whimsical examples. It could be said therefore that Cornwall has become a jumbled museum of country houses. This is because many have grown piecemeal, some distance from the ebb and flow of architectural fashions and driven by half-interested patrons and enthusiastic local builders. Many houses boast an equal measure of aesthetic quality and lovable eccentricity, not having been unduly spoilt by generations of improvers because generations of absentee landlords have capitalised on their mineral wealth and as a result have focused on their bases east of the river Tamar. My conclusion is that Pevsner's opening line in his 1951 edition of Cornwall unfairly underpins the rest of the volume. Cornwall may not be the most reliable gauge for architectural excellence, but it does have a fine collection of country houses that are not only 'lovable' and 'moving' but also tell a story of continuity that is both endearing and poignant.

We are fortunate in Cornwall to have a relatively good survival rate of country seats. Betjeman, again, is perhaps the best person to explain how the 20th century treated these heritage assets. In the opening chapter of *Ghastly Good Taste*, entitled 'An Apostrophe to one of the Landed Gentry', he immerses the reader in a witty yet prosaic history of the archetypal country house and its owners, who have seen fickle fashions and transient tastes come and go. He reflects on life-changing developments such as the coming of the railway, the motor car, the telephone and eventually the cluster-fly. He heralds the loss of the servants, the disposal of the family wealth and the eventual sale of the peripheries of the estate for new development. He concludes with the estate gates being flung open and, as the owners grind their teeth, they welcome tourists as they move their belongings into the redundant servants' quarters.

Notes

1. John Betjeman, *Cornwall: a Shell Guide* (London, 1964), p.9.
2. Pevsner (1951), p.11.
3. John Betjeman, *Ghastly Good Taste: Or, a Depressing Story of the Rise and Fall of English Architecture* (London, 1933).
4. Paul Holden, *Lanhydrock* (Stroud, 2007).
5. Paul Holden, 'How Soon the Cornish Renaissance?', *Cornish Buildings Group Newsletter* (2007), p.5.

6 Philibert de l'Orme, *La Premier tome de l'architecture* (1568).
7 Pevsner (2014), pp.211–12.
8 Similar features had already been used to great affect at Apethorpe Hall, Nottinghamshire; Canterbury Quad at St John's College, Oxford and the Queen's House at Greenwich.
9 Tim Mowl, *Gardens of Cornwall* (Stroud, 2005), p.248
10 Michael Trinick, 'The Great House of Stowe', *Journal of the Royal Institution of Cornwall*, Vol. 8, (1974), pp.90–108
11 Paul Holden, 'Pencarrow', *Country Life*, 18 August 2010.
12 Paul Holden, 'Trewithen and the Brettingham Plans', *Georgian Group Journal*, Volume XXI, (2013), pp.58–72
13 'Jaunt to Cornwall August – September 1792', *The Journal of James Boswell 1784–94*, Vol. XVIII (privately published in USA, 1933), p.158.
14 Lanhydrock Accounts 1772–90 (Private Collection)
15 CRO FS 3/1126/1,2. 'A Commonplace Life', Memoirs of Sarah Gregor.

Gothic Survival or Revival in Cornwall?

Patrick Newberry

With its rugged coasts, stark moors and mysterious culture, Cornwall appears for many as a dark place. Architecurally this mood conjures up the Gothic, perhaps situated on brooding cliff-tops or across isolated, furtive, commons. The truth however is somewhat different. Most sensible Cornishmen favoured more protected sheltered coombes away from often hostile weather patterns, their choice of architecture being somewhat eclectic and, more often than not, following contemporary fashions. However, as in most counties, the Gothic style has been an important part of Cornwall's architectural development; this chapter will explore the impact of the Gothic style and question whether it survived despite the prevailing popularity of Classicism or was revived during the 18th and 19th centuries.

For many years orthodox architectural historians have held firm to the belief that the Gothic style died out in the 17th century, only to be revived during the 18th.[1] This renewal of Gothic sensibilities, referred to as Gothick, differed from the medieval masons structural use of stone, moving towards a decorator's style whereby ornament was worked-up in plaster or lighter material for adornment. For Cornwall, however, Gothic lingered longer than in many parts of the country suggesting that survival may have merged undetectably into revival. Evidence for this contention can be seen in three notable Cornish buildings.

First, the east-facing elevation of the gatehouse at Lanhydrock presents to the outside world a Renaissance image, admittedly already out dated by 1651 when it was completed. But pass through the wide arch and examine the inward (west-facing) facade and a fine example of late Gothic architecture appears, complete with blind tracery.[2] Speculatively the two distinct facades might relate to its owner, Lord Robartes, putting forward an expression of modernity yet inwardly acknowledging the past, possibly trying to suggest ancient family roots. It is equally likely, however, that the stone masons were still versed in the Gothic style and, faced with the need to cover both elevations of the gatehouse, reverted to the Gothic for its lesser front.

The second, the porch at Trewan Hall, near St Columb, was built, most likely, within a decade of the Lanhydrock gatehouse, its similar Gothic detailing suggests that it was designed and/or built by the same artisans.³ The third is the Church of King Charles the Martyr in Falmouth, mostly built in 1661. Few new churches were built in Cornwall during the late 17th century and this important church, partly funded by the King, may well have been built with thin late-perpendicular Gothic details during the febrile climate of the Restoration as a statement of support for the Royalist cause. However, before reading too much into this stylistic match, it is worth recalling a point made by Howard Colvin '…apart from St Paul's Covent Garden, what is now Marlborough House Chapel, and a small church at Hale in Hampshire, rebuilt in 1631–2, no completely classical church was built in England until after the Great Fire'.⁴ In that context, King Charles the Martyr is not that unusual and does not, as such, suggest that Cornwall was significantly out of line with taste in the rest of the country.

Proponents of the theory that Gothic survived into the 18th century argue that the limited scope of local masons and their belief in historical traditions maintained its momentum. In his book West Britons, Mark Stoyle considered that Cornish resistance to a new Prayer Book in the 16th century and fervent support for the Royalist cause during the Civil War had less to do with the principle of Latinised liturgy or indeed the Divine Right of Kings and more to do with an English Prayer Book and a Puritan Government being seen as instruments of Cornish Anglicisation.⁵ Following the same logic, it is possible that some Cornishmen may have held on to the Gothic style, seeing the alternative new fashion for Classicism as an imposition of an alien, English, culture. Such argument for a Gothic Survival does not mean that Cornwall lagged behind when adopting new architectural styles as Stowe near Kilkhampton and Newton Ferrers near Callington prove.

Although the evidence cited above supports survival of Gothic up to the latter part of the 17th century, the argument for Gothic merging undetectably into revival in the 18th century does not hold up well in Cornwall, given the absence of late 17th and early 18th century Gothic work. Markedly absent are examples of Gothic work by the contemporaries of Christopher Wren, Nicholas Hawksmoor or John Vanbrugh. But if the thread of Gothic dies in Cornwall during the late 17th century, revival happens quite early. Throughout the country early examples of Gothic Revival tend to focus around follies and the Gothicising of a number of houses in the period between 1718 and 1745.⁶ One example might be Pentillie Castle, on the banks of the river Tamar at Pillaton, where an 18th century drawing suggests that the flanking wings of the house featured Gothic windows. Although many writers, including Pevsner, have described Cornwall as being generally slow to adapt to new architectural styles, the evidence of the Gothick Revival suggests that this may not be so.

Probably the earliest reliable examples in Cornwall are St Michael's Mount's Rococo Gothick Blue Drawing Room, completed between 1733 and 1744,⁷ and Werrington church (Fig. 1 and 2), dismantled in 1742 by Sir William Morice and rebuilt on a new site in the Rococo Gothick style. Both are nationally early examples, the work at Werrington being carried out some twenty years before a similar church moving exercise at Croome Court in Worcestershire by Capability Brown and Robert Adam. The buildings are connected in that the owner of St Michael's Mount, Sir John St Aubyn, married Catherine, Sir William Morice's sister, whose mother Catherine

Herbert was the sister of the 9th Earl of Pembroke, a noted amateur architect. Although no documentary evidence has been found, it is tempting to hypothesise that the St Aubyn and Morice architectural precociousness was inspired by the architect Earl who, although he mostly worked in a Palladian style, was closely associated with Roger Morris, a significant player in the resurgence of the Gothick style.[8] It is of further note that Pembroke worked at Castle Hill in Devon, only fifty miles from Werrington. Slightly later, in 1747, the Edgcumbes of Mount Edgcumbe amalgamated elements of two demolished Plymouth churches into a Gothick ruin, modified the corner towers of their mansion in 1749 in a Tudor Gothic style, and erected a simple Gothick tower in 1750 as a navigation mark at Penlee Point on the shore of Plymouth Sound.

These three examples feature early in the renaissance of Gothick fashions and, more importantly, predate Horace Walpole's remodelling of Strawberry Hill. Not only does this prove that Cornish patrons could be progressive in their choice of architectural style but also suggests that they drew on influences outside of the county, perhaps whilst in London serving as members of parliament. Friendships too were an important influence on style. Horace Walpole, for example, was a close acquaintance of Richard Edgcumbe, 2nd Baron, whose work at Mount Edgcumbe preceded the much fêted work at Strawberry Hill. It is of note that two men with Cornish connections had some influence on Walpole's masterpiece, but did not bring their Gothick influence to Cornwall. The first was Pope's Twickenham neighbour John Robartes who became 4th Earl Radnor but did not inherit the Lanhydrock estates. Radnor refashioned his own house, Radnor House, in the Gothick style some years prior to Strawberry Hill. Another contemporary Cornish architect manqué, Thomas Pitt, was consulted by Walpole on the design of the Gallery at Strawberry Hill and designed a Gothick Cottage at Park Place, Henley on Thames. Despite spending time at Boconnoc, his estate near Lostwithiel, and designing buildings in Cornwall, he seemingly never tried his hand at the pointed style in the county.

The most prolific exponent of the Gothick style in Cornwall was Thomas Edwards.

Fig. 1. *The Blue Drawing room at St Michael's Mount.* Eric Berry.

Fig. 2. *West end of Werrington church showing Gothic detailing.* Author.

Better known for his Palladian designs at Carclew, Tehidy and Nanswhyden, Edwards was inspired by the Gothick style for some of his country house works, most notably at Trelowarren in the late 1750s. Two more speculative Edwards connections are at Mount Edgcumbe for whose owner during the late 1750s and early 1760s he was recorded as having carried out work, perhaps the Rococo Gothick decoration of the central hall, (Fig.3) and the pavilion or summer house built on axis with the garden front of Carclew. This latter building (which appears to date from between 1740 and 1760 when the mansion was reworked) is a wonderful example of Rococo Gothick, many of the details clearly inspired by the published works of Batty Langley.[9] Edwards work was not confined to the country house, his church work included the reconstruction of St Gluvias in Penryn, a new tower and west end to St Mary's, Truro, and a complete rebuild of St Michael's, Helston, all of which deployed a weak Gothick to some extent reminiscent of the earlier Gothick work of Hawksmoor and Wren.

The momentum for Gothick did not wane during the latter part of the 18th century. Between 1773 and 1775 two Picturesque Gothick 'central plan' castles were built, Tregenna Castle at St Ives for the Stephens family and Acton Castle near Perranuthnoe for the Stackhouse family.[10] Much conjecture has developed over their authorship. Lake's Parochial History of Cornwall suggests that 'Mr Wood of Bath' was the architect of Tregenna Castle.[11] It has been suggested that this 'Mr Wood' was not John Wood the Younger of Bath, but actually William Wood of Truro, although another school-of-thought has drawn convincing similarities between both castles and John Wood's work, John Wood having a connection with St Ives through the Knill Monument and his design for the almshouses, both being built on land belonging to Samuel Stephens of Tregenna.[12]

Other late 18th century Gothick works include a prospect tower in the landscape gardens at Cotehele, which was possibly built for the visit of King George III in 1789.

Fig. 3
Engraving by Thomas Allom of Mount Edgcumbe showing 18th century Gothic detailing to the outside of the central hall. Author's collection.

Fig. 4
Caerhayes castle an exemplar of Picturesque Gothic. Author

This triangular tower (perhaps inspired by the symbolism made popular by the likes of Thomas Tresham and his contemporaries) belongs to the group of towers built by Henry Hoare at Stourhead and Charles Hamilton at Painshill in the 1760s and 1770s. Catchfrench, a crenelated, Picturesque Gothick country house near Hessenford, was designed c.1780 by Charles Rawlinson, a Lostwithiel architect. Some idea of the house's original appearance can be gleaned from a Red Book produced for the estate by Humphrey Repton, shewing a largely symmetrical and classical Georgian house in Gothick dress. Also in south east Cornwall, attractive, if unchallenging, are later Gothick houses built at Restormel and Stoketon.

Enthusiasm for the Picturesque Gothick style continued into the 19th century as prosperity from mining, banking and industry enabled Cornish patrons to commission architects with a national reputation. At Port Eliot, St Germans, the Eliot family embarked on a lengthy remodelling of their seat, first, sometime before 1793, by John Johnson, a London based architect, and then by John Soane. Despite including the impressive round drawing room, Johnson's work was roundly dismissed by Humphrey Repton as tame 'Islington Gothic', a point not contested by Soane who later enhanced the Drawing Room, remodelled the north front and built the stables. In 1829 Henry Harrison resolved the vexed question of giving the house an entrance hall worthy of its status, in a Tudor Gothic style.

These efforts were modest compared with the early 19th century construction of Caerhays Castle by John Bettesworth Trevanion (Fig.4). His choice of architect was the Prince Regent's favourite, John Nash, an expensive choice that was subsequently to ruin him. Nash had started building faux-castles in the 1790s, an early example being

Fig. 5
Moorswater Lodge, Liskeard, lithograph from Twycross's Mansions of England and Wales; Cornwall, showing the view across the park to this unusual Moorish Gothic house. Author's collection.

Luscombe Castle in Devon. Although reputedly not a particular fan of the Gothic style, he recognised that it was a popular amongst his clients and so produced a whole string of crenelated mansions. He was more convincing in his massing than the Adams brothers, although his Gothic houses generally lack the Gothic "spikiness" achieved by James Wyatt, who made one brief Gothic foray into Cornwall, building a new church at Kea, for R.L. Gwatkin of Killiow.[13]

The craze for castle building continued into the new century. On the banks of the Tamar at Pentillie, the Corytons commissioned two unlikely Gothic architects, William Wilkins and his son, also William, to extend the late 17th century house. Wilkins Jnr is better known today for his classical work,[14] whilst his father had, in the 1790s, rebuilt Donnington Hall in Leicestershire for the Earl of Moira, as a symmetrical classical box clothed in Gothick dress – a not very promising credential for an architect worthy of Pentillie's stunning position. R.W. Liscombe, biographer of Wilkins Jnr, notes that the architects were introduced to the Corytons by Humphrey Repton, who had already included a romantic Gothick design for the house in his Pentillie Red Book.[15] Repton's design however did not find favour with the Corytons. Wilkins father and son produced a very different design for extending and remodelling the existing house drawing on picturesque massing, although still featuring detailing that was archaeologically incorrect, similar to that used by Wilkins Snr at Donnington.

From Pentillie, Repton progressed to Tregothnan where the 4th Viscount Falmouth also rejected the landscape gardener's architectural aspirations turning instead to the Wilkinses. Repton could be the link here, however, Wilkins Jnr was building a Gothic house at Dalmeny, near Edinburgh, for the Earl of Roseberry, a fellow member with Lord Falmouth of the Society of Dilettanti. Tregothnan was an even more asymmetric and dramatic composition than Pentillie and presages the 19th century fashion for powerful irregular Gothic houses. As J.P. Neale is his *Views of Seats* remarked 'Its irregularity of form and variety of enrichment have been adapted with minute attention; the ornamented battlements and richly decorated turrets have a pleasing effect; the sculptured compartments, and mullioned windows co-operate to produce the utmost uniformity of design in the magnificent edifice'.[16] Tregothnan was the most impressive mansion in Cornwall of its day, its style was Tudor Gothic, a point addressed by Stockdale 'Its irregularity of form, and variety of ornament, closely resemble the style of buildings erected during the reign of Henry VII'.[17]

Houses of the scale of Caerhays, Pentillie, Port Eliot and Tregothnan placed Cornwall in the vanguard of Regency Gothic country house building. Other, more modest, houses in the Gothic style appeared, such as Trebursye (c.1820) by Sir Jeffrey Wyatville; Moorswater Lodge (1830), a pretty Picturesque Gothic, almost Moorish, house, built to the west of Liskeard (Fig.5); Luxstowe in Liskeard (1831–2) by George Wightwick, for William Glencross, a wealthy merchant and, perhaps Cornwall's most extraordinary Gothic house, Place at Fowey, where a mediaeval house with 18th century Picturesque Gothick additions was extensively reworked between 1813 and 1845. Gothic also started to be used for civic buildings, examples include St Day clock tower (1830) and the Grammar School and Grylls memorial at Helston (1834) both by Wightwick. Churches too favoured a watery 'Commissioners' Gothic' – Chasewater, Penzance, Redruth and St Day, all by Charles Hutchens of Torpoint, being good examples. While these churches lack the vigour of later 19th century Gothic architecture, they are not without their charm. A similar stylistically weak form of Gothic was used for some of the vast number of non conformist chapels built in the first half of the 19th century.

The 1830s and 1840s saw the emergence of the last great phase of the Revival, Ecclesiologists Gothic. Led by A.W.N. Pugin its philosophy was embeded in the belief that Gothic church architecture would only work when church ritual returned to its mediaeval forms.[18] Hence, its architectural expression was to purify Gothic to archaeological exactitude, basing itself mostly in the Early English and Decorated periods and thereby replacing the flimsiness of earlier revival Gothick. The Ecclesiologist Bishop of Exeter, Henry Phillpotts, ensured that Ecclesiology had a strong impact in Cornwall, even if Pugin and the mainstream Ecclesiologist architects, such as William Butterfield, Richard Cromwell Carpenter and Benjamin Ferrey, completed little work in the county.[19] Architects who worked closely with Ecclesiological principles such as George Edmund Street, John Loughborough Pearson and William White (who set up a practice in the County), were very active in Cornwall, Street building his first ever church, St Mary's, Par (Fig.6), Pearson building St John, Devoran, (1855) and William White rebuilding St Hilary after a fire (1853–5) and a new church of St Philip and St James, Maryfield, Antony (1864–71). As the century progressed so the Gothic style for church building gathered momentum, as elsewhere in the country, into what Professor Mordaunt Crook described as the Eclectic phase.[20] This phase of development is epit-

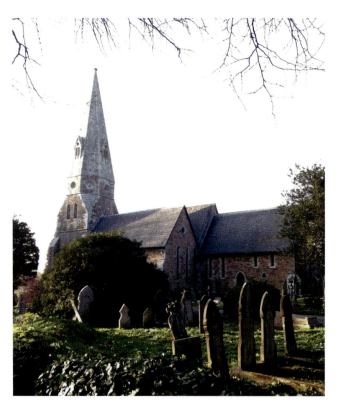

Fig. 6
St Mary's church, Par, George Edmund Street's first full Gothic Revival church.
Author.

omised by the putative Bishop's Palace at St Columb by White and St Faith's House of Mercy, near Lostwithiel, by Street, both built in uncompromising Early English and Decorated styles and both undoubtedly heartily approved of by the Ecclesiologists, as well as the new cathedral in Truro by John Loughborough Pearson. In the realms of civic architecture Gothic does not manifest itself as greatly in Cornwall as it does elsewhere, Launceston Town Hall being a rare example.

Despite the 18th century enthusiasm for the Gothick country house style, the percentage of houses built in the 19th century in Cornwall was significantly lower than the national average.[21] However, some houses were built or extended in the prevailing fashion, the most notable examples being Tregothnan by Lewis Vulliamy, the masterful extension to St Michael's Mount by James Piers St Aubyn and some lesser houses including Tregenna House at Michaelstowe, Penstowe House near Kilkhampton and Lewarne and Treverbyn Vean, both near Liskeard. It is apparent that after the 1870s, the pace of the Gothic style slowed and by the early 20th century it dwindled to a trickle.

This chapter has explored the argument that while we might view Gothic as a continuing tradition across the country as a whole, in Cornwall, it sustained well into the 17th century but ceased to be used actively by the century's close. By contrast, 18th century Cornish patrons were far from laggards in the way they adopted and adapted Gothic styles as they came back into fashion, an enthusiasm that continued well into the 19th century, with fine examples of domestic and ecclesiastical Gothic buildings. Gothic during the 20th century was more benign, the century's main achievements including St Michael's church, Newquay (1909) by Sir Ninian Comper (the last significant Gothic church in the county, the tower was not added until 1961 by Sebastian Comper), some Gothick reworking of parts of Catchfrench (1913) by Alfred Cornelius (although he removed the battlements from the main part of the house) and the end of refurbishment works at St Michael's Mount (1927). Thereafter the Gothic stream seems to disappear

But have we really seen the end of Gothic in Cornwall? As the 21st century dawns, there are signs that the style is still in use and that the stream may continue, albeit as a trickle. A new restaurant and shop at the Duchy Nursery near Lostwithiel takes the form of a Reptonian rustic lodge (Fig.7), a Gothic hen house adorns the grounds of a

Fig. 7
Duchy Nursery, café and shop, Lostwithiel. Picturesque Gothic for the 21st century. Author.

beautifully restored mediaeval house near Liskeard and a tea temple based on a design of Capability Brown is in the planning for a garden in south-east Cornwall. All proof perhaps that the Gothic has not yet left us for good.

A recent writer on the topic of survival versus revival, Dr Giles Worsley, took the view that we should treat Gothic as a continuing tradition, albeit with interruptions on the journey, he wrote '…instead of being a brief, rather frivolous episode of the 1750s, Gothic should be seen as a continuous undercurrent in English architecture from the sixteenth century…we should perhaps be talking of the continuing Gothic tradition'.[22] These comments describe well the Cornish experience.

Notes

1. Charles L. Eastlake, *A History of the Gothic Revival* (London, 1872) was firmly of the opinion that Gothic architecture had died out in England during the 17th century and was revived by Horace Walpole, Batty Langley and their contemporaries in the mid-18th. Kenneth Clark, *The Gothic Revival* (London, 1928), p.13, considered '…a tiny stream of the Gothic tradition…was never lost, but flowed unbroken from Henry VII's chapel to the Houses of Parliament'. Howard Colvin, 'Gothic Revival and Survival', *Architectural Review*, ciii, (1948), pp.91–8, revised in *Essays in English Architectural History* (London and New Haven, 1999), pp.217–45, concurred, but added that the continuum was in part due to local traditions and family masons copying details of, for example, medieval church towers. Professor J. Mordaunt Crook in his introduction to the revised Charles L Eastlake, *A History of the Gothic Revival* (Leicester and New York, 1978), p.27 was less committed, he wrote 'Trying to track down a chronological watershed between the survival and revival of Gothic is like chasing a will o' the wisp'.
2. Paul Holden, 'How Soon the Cornish Renaissance?', *Cornish Buildings Group Newsletter* (2007), p.5
3. Paul Holden, '"Situation, Contrivance, Strength and Beauty": the creation of Lanhydrock House 1620–45', *Royal*

Institution of Cornwall, (2005), pp.32–44. Elsewhere in the country the use of secular Gothic had dwindled rapidly by the mid-17th century, notable exceptions being certain Oxford and Cambridge Colleges, a handful of bishop's palaces and a few private houses.

4. Colvin, *op cite*. p.218.
5. Mark Stoyle, *West Britons: Cornish Identities and the Early Modern British State* (Exeter, 2002).
6. Early examples of the Gothick Revival style include Shotover Park (1718), Clearwell Castle (1728), Alfred's Hall at Cirencester Park (1732) and James Gibbs's Gothick temple at Stowe (1741). Gothick reworking of houses gathers pace in the early 1740s with additions to Welbeck Abbey (1742), Radway Grange (1744), Belhus (1745), Inveraray Castle (1745) and Horace Walpole's iconic Strawberry Hill, where Gothick work started in 1749.
7. Peter Herring, *An Archaeological Evaluation of St Michael's Mount*, (Cornwall, 1993).
8. Examples being Clearwell castle (1728) and Inverary castle (1745–60).
9. B. and T. Langley, *Gothic Architecture Improved By Rules and Proportions* (London, 1747).
10. Eastlake, *op cite*. p.51. Professor Mordaunt Crook suggests that Picturesque Gothick castles were generally built according to three plans – courtyard plans, central plans and asymmetric plans. Notable examples include Richard Payne Knight's Downton Castle (1772), Robert Adam's Culzean Castle (1777), James Wyatt's Kew (1802) and Ashridge (1808), Robert Smirke's Lowther Castle (1806) and the Elliot's Taymouth Castle (1806).
11. Lake, *Parochial History of Cornwall* (Truro, 1870)
12. *Pers comms* Paul Holden and Nick Cahill 2015. John Stackhouse was a habitué of Bath
13. Little is recorded about Wyatt's church, but it proved unsatisfactory and was demolished in 1895.
14. Such as the National Gallery, Downing College, University College London and Northington Grange.
15. R.W. Liscombe, *William Wilkins 1778–1839* (London,1980).
16. J.P. Neale, *Views of the Seats of Noblemen and Gentlemen, in England, Wales, Scotland and Ireland, Volume 1*.(London 1818).
17. F.W.L.Stockdale, *Excursions in the County of Cornwall* (London 1824), p.56
18. Although Pugin was an inspiration to the later Gothic Revival, he was nlot an Ecclesiologist.
19. Pugin did, however, have one work in Cornwall, a robust Gothic rectory at Lanteglos-by-Camelford, built for the Reverend John Rouse Bloxham (now a hotel). For details of its gestation, see Margaret Belcher (ed.), *The Collected Letters of A.W.N. Pugin*, (Oxford, 2003), vol.2 (1843–5). I am indebted to Michael Swift for kindly reminding me of Pugin's foray into Cornwall. It is unclear whether Pugin ever visited the site or whether he simply provided the designs for execution by a local architect or builder. Butterfield too worked in the county carrying out a few restorations and building a rectory at St Mawgan in his typically tough muscular Gothic. This is a work of some distinction and in its massing, composition and detailing displays Butterfield's mastery of the Gothic style.
20. Eastlake, *op cite*. p.16.
21. Across the UK, just under half of all significant country houses built during Victoria's reign were built in the Gothic style. In Cornwall, the corresponding figure is nearer one third.
22. G. Worsley, *Classical Architecture in Britain; The Heroic Age* (London 1995), p.175.

A Victorian Vision Re-discovered: the stained glass windows of St Carantoc, Cornwall[1]

Michael G. Swift

The restoration of St Carantoc parish church at Crantock was one of the most ambitious in late Victorian Cornwall; one commentator has rightly described it as 'a little masterpiece'.[2] This chapter places the incumbent's scheme for the stained glass windows within the architectural and liturgical context of the church, and examines the relationships between his scheme and that of Bishop Edward White Benson for the windows of his new Truro Cathedral (1887–1910), the high-water mark of the Gothic Revival in Cornwall.[3]

When Father George Metford Parsons (1851–1924) arrived at Crantock in 1894 (Fig.1) he found a parish church with a venerable history reduced to 'something near to a mere picturesque ruin'.[4] Such was the drive and determination of Father George (as he was known locally) that within eight years the Vicarage House, glebe barn and the medieval collegiate church were all restored or completely rebuilt. He possessed enormous energy to achieve such results in so short a space of time, as well as abundant fundraising skills.

The architect entrusted with the church's restoration was Edmund Harold Sedding (1863–1921). After opening his practice in Plymouth in 1891, Sedding soon established a reputation throughout the Diocese of Truro for his sympathetic church restorations and his informed knowledge of medieval Cornish ecclesiological architecture.[5] A High Anglican, like his father and uncle,[6] he took as his main principle the Tractarian concern 'to so order the worship in an Anglican Church and its surroundings as to proclaim the Catholicity of Anglicanism and its fitness to stand alongside the great churches of Christendom as an equal partner, sharing apostolic faith and order.'[7]

With such grounding in the Gothic Revival, the architect was also 'a careful repairer of old fabric, adept at commission-

Fig. 1
Father George Metford Parsons, incumbent 1894–1924.
Author.

ing new artists and craftsmen, and advocating the use of local materials'.[8] St Carantoc's restoration started in 1897 and the church was reopened in 1902.

> The principal beauty of St Carantoc is its very rich High Church fittings, dating mainly from 1897–1907. They include a splendid screen with coving, loft and rood, which incorporates a few medieval parts. There are fine parclose screens, rich sanctuary panelling, reredos, timber sedilia, and lavish stalls including four modern misericords. The pews have good carved ends in the late medieval manner. The largely renewed roofs have fine colouring above the rood and the sanctuary.[9]

This authoritative summary of Sedding's restoration has however one astounding omission: it contains no reference to the fifteen new stained glass windows that were an integral part of the restored church, and completed, together with many other internal fixtures and fittings, by 1907.[10]

Crantock's new windows were unique among parish churches of Cornwall in two crucial respects: all of the windows were part of a complete didactic scheme compiled by Father George,[11] and all designed and executed by one stained glass artist, Charles Edward Tute.[12] The pivotal role of these stained glass windows in Cornwall's Gothic Revival can now been told for the first time.

Father George made no concessions in his High Anglican beliefs,[13] being part of the tradition of Anglo-Catholic priests that flourished in the new Diocese of Truro after 1877. Rather than seeking donors for the windows and leaving the choice of the subject-matter to them (the normal practice in Victorian restorations), he insisted on adherence to his integrated didactic scheme, which was a robust Anglo-Catholic response to the challenges of both the Low Anglican Church and the Non-conformists.[14]

Stained glass didactic schemes are a common feature of ecclesiastical windows from medieval times onwards to the present day. Whatever their age and scale, all such integrated schemes have certain features in common. Firstly they present multi-layered theological ideas, religious narratives and personages in a coherent and logical sequence. Secondly, such glazing schemes utilize the features of the building's architectural space, and relate the iconography of the windows to the functions of liturgy and worship within that space. Thirdly, the glazing schemes have an overall artistic unity and design. Lastly, they have a didactic purpose: besides enhancing the worshipful atmosphere they were also intended to teach and instruct.

With the possible exception of the Pole-Carew estate church at Maryfield, Antony,[15] the only Cornish example of a didactic scheme was the windows at John Loughborough Pearson's new cathedral at Truro. This monumental scheme for over eighty windows was originally designed by Bishop Benson in 1879. Stressing the need for theological coherence and liturgical relevance, it was published in full at the cathedral's consecration in 1887. To ensure artistic unity, the commission for the entire set of the new cathedral's windows was awarded to the prestigious London studio of Clayton and Bell. When Crantock's restoration commenced, Truro cathedral was already ten years old and more than thirty of its windows had been inserted.[16] As will be shown

Fig. 2
The parish church of St Carantoc, Crantock.
P. Holden

there are striking parallels between the intentions and iconography of both schemes.

Crantock church's very unusual architectural layout, with a three aisled chancel, north and south transepts, and a single aisled nave (Fig.2) reflects its origins as a medieval Collegiate church.[17] As with Truro cathedral, the basic ground form of the building is a cruciform shape, presenting the opportunity to use the glass in 'four great windows' at the extremities of the east, south, west and north arms to portray themes of major theological significance. In Truro, the three rose windows depict the Holy Trinity, with a Te Deum Christ in Glory in the Quire east window. Both Crantock and Truro schemes utilise the symbolism of the cross in the shape of the building to focus on its theme of Christ as the Son of God, and integrate religious iconography with architectural form and liturgical function.

The first of Crantock's four great windows, in the north transept, depicts three scenes of the Fall of Man and the Expulsion from the Garden. The 'right-to-left' layout directs the viewer towards the next great window in the sequence, the tower west, which depicts the Incarnation. Father George's recommended route then moves back to the south transept, but he encouraged the viewer to pause at the rood screen. Although this is not technically part of the stained glass scheme, contemporary documents place the rood screen together with the four great windows as an integral scheme to illustrate 'the five principal Mysteries of Human Redemption.'[18] The south transept window depicts three scenes of the four witnesses to the Resurrection.

Proceeding through the screen, the chancel south window is not part of the 'four

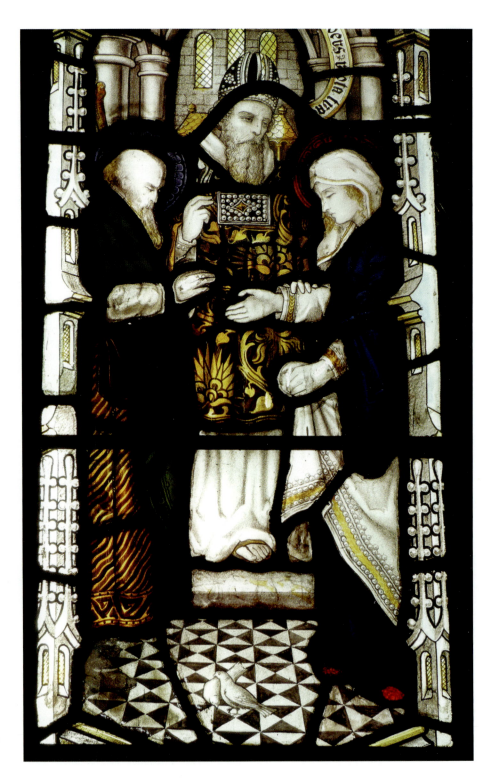

Fig. 3
Lady chapel south: marrige of Mary and Joseph.
P. Holden

great windows', but Christ's charge to Peter, deliberately placed in the liturgically significant position at the sanctuary rail, emphasises the principle of Apostolic Succession stretching right back to the authority of Christ's commission to the first Bishop of Rome.

The chancel east window is the climax of Father George's scheme for the four great windows. Both Crantock and Truro cathedral's east windows share the subject of a Te Deum portrayal of Christ in Glory surrounded by all the company of Heaven (Fig 6). Below Christ at Crantock is a crowned Blessed Virgin Mary, a symbol of Anglo-Catholic iconography.

The second part of Father George's didactic scheme is the three windows for the Lady chapel. Here the subject-matter is totally concerned with Marian iconography, far more than is usual in Anglican parish churches, and has no parallel in the Truro scheme. These images are supplemented by the roof bosses, which are Types for the Incarnation and the Blessed Virgin Mary.[19] Father George's Anglo-Catholic intention was to portray the role traditionally given to her by the church as one predestined to bring about the redemption of man from the 'sin of Eve'.[20] The two south wall windows contain early episodes in her life taken from the medieval source-text 'The Golden Legend' and the Gospels: - the father Joachim with the infant Mary; the mother Anne instructing Mary to read; and Mary as a young woman in the Temple: the rare

Fig. 4
North nave: Saints Carantoc and Patrick.
P. Holden

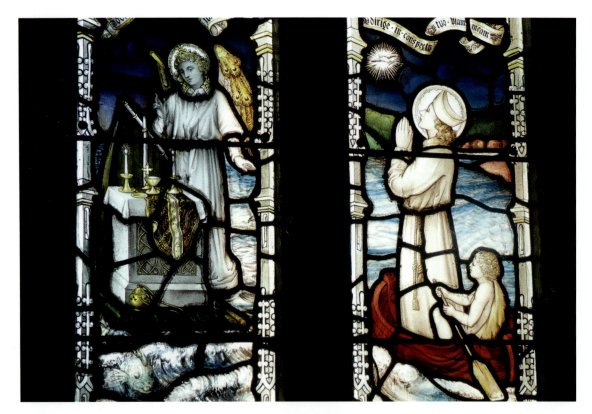

Fig. 5
South nave: the legend of St Carantoc
P. Holden

Fig. 6
Opposite page
Chancel east: Christ in Majesty.
P. Holden

subject in windows of the marriage of Joseph and Mary (Fig 3); the Annunciation to Mary; and the Visitation. The final image of the Madonna and Child with the kneeling figures of St John the Evangelist and St Joseph in the east window forms the dominant visual focus for this whole architectural and liturgical space.

One of St Carantoc's strangest architectural features is the contrast between the narrow nave and the three-aisled choir.[21] Father George's scheme for the nave windows identified four narratives from the patronal saint's life. 'The Lives of the Saints were not based on earlier historic records, but on local folklore and contemporary views of what a saint should be like.'[22] Father George's windows are a fascinating example of what he thought a pre-medieval saint should be like in a late Victorian didactic scheme!

On the north side of the nave a youthful St Carantoc as a Celtic hermit preacher lands on a typical north Cornish coastline while the south nave shows the saint, now a deacon, in a coracle following a floating altar complete with a guardian angel, candles, chalice, paten and censer – a robust statement of Anglo-Catholic ritual status.[23] (Fig 5). Also in the south nave St Carantoc, now a priest, converts the local community at Tintagel.

The final window in the St Carantoc narrative, situated in the north nave, poses considerable interpretive problems to the modern viewer (Fig 4). The scene shows a seated priest with a written scroll inscribed 'Seanghus Mor' or the Senchas Mar, an early Irish compilation of law-texts written in the seventh and eighth centuries. He is presumably St Carantoc, and the bishop opposite, holding a blank scroll, could therefore be St Patrick. So, the window can be read as showing the legendary role played by St Carantoc in the harmonisation of Christianity with secular law in Ireland.

One problem in this interpretation of the window is that the priest's face is obviously a photographic likeness of an actual person, now identified as that of Revd R.A. Suckling (1842–1917), incumbent at St Alban's Holborn in 1882.[24] Sedding's uncle, John Dando Sedding, was churchwarden of St Alban's Holborn for ten years until his death in 1891.[25] Suckling succeeded one of the founders of the Oxford Movement, Edward Bouverie Pusey, as warden of Ascot Priory's Society of the Most Holy Trinity, the centre for the Community of the Sisters of Charity and the first community of Anglican nuns.[26] In his later life, Pusey was a frequent summer visitor to Crantock. Thus, there must be an intended Tractarian sub-text to this window.

High Churchmen like Father George and Bishop Benson were faced with what they believed was the problem of combining the tradition of 'Celtic' Christianity with that of the Apostolic Succession of the Church of Rome.[27] All this evidence supports a further reading of this window, where the 'Celtic' tradition (represented by St Carantoc) and the Roman tradition (represented by St Patrick) were reconciled. It is easy to see the appeal of such a theme to a Ritualist like Father George.

One of the main functions of integrated window schemes is to relate iconography to liturgy and architectural space. At Crantock the font is positioned between the last two Nave windows, showing the conversion of the local population (a process that would involve immediate baptism) and the transition from the Celtic to the Augustinian churches (involved the adoption of Augustinian sacraments, notably baptism). So, one function of Father George's windows scheme was in effect to create a baptistry space. Bishop Benson's scheme for the windows in Truro Cathedral placed great emphasis on the theme of Christian and particularly Cornish mission,[28] and at the cathedral's consecration in 1887, its baptistry windows showing four Cornish Celtic saints were already inserted.[29] The parallels between the Truro windows and the portrayals of St Carantoc confirm that Father George had an intimate knowledge of the cathedral scheme.

C.E. Tute's windows at Crantock were not in the top artistic league, but they were cheaper than Truro's.[30] The average cost per window was about £50[31] (nave windows by Clayton and Bell at Truro cathedral were £100). At Crantock the windows have no memorial inscriptions, as the normal Victorian practice of recording the names of the dedicatees within the window would have distracted from the scheme's didactic intentions. Also, potential donors responded to Father George's appeal astonishingly quickly. Lastly there seems to have been complete agreement between the donors and incumbent on the choice of subject-matter for the windows, as happened with Benson's scheme at Truro.

Besides imparting an artistic unity to the church's interior, the themes of Father George's scheme are intimately connected with the architecture and liturgy of the church. These themes are an emphatic Anglo-Catholic statement of the place of this parish church within the Church of England at the turn of the century, being concerned not only with deep theological issues but also referencing local Cornish Celtic heritage. There can be no doubt that Father George was profoundly influenced by Bishop Benson's window scheme at Truro, the most important Gothic Revival building in Cornwall.

In 1894, Father George Metford Parsons started his thirty year curacy of Saint Carantoc church dedicated to the fulfilment of his vision to restore this historic building to its former glory. The restoration of the church would eventually cost over £11,000, raised from far and wide as a response to the Priest's eloquence and tenacity.[32] His restoration of St Carantoc church is a fitting and lasting memorial to a truly remarkable priest and to the spirit of the Gothic Revival. It is appropriate that the architect E.H. Sedding should have the last word : 'The old collegiate church once again possesses its stalls, screens, coloured glass and carved imagery, and is therefore redeemed and put right again in the sight of those who reverence God's sanctuary.'[33]

Notes

1. Michael G. Swift and Jeni Stewart-Smith, 'A Victorian Vision Rediscovered', *Journal of the Royal Institute of Cornwall*, (2014), pp.25–41.
2. Peter Beacham, *Journal of the Victorian Society*, (March, 2014), p.7.
3. Pevsner (2014), pp.662–7.
4. H. Miles Brown, *The Parish Church of St Carantoc*, (Newquay, 1996), p.7.
5. Edmund H. Sedding, *Norman Architecture in Cornwall*, (London, 1909), p.71.
6. James Stevens Curl, *Victorian Architecture – Diversity and Invention*, (Reading, 2007), p.336.
7. H. Miles Brown *The Catholic Revival in Cornish Anglicanism*, (St Winnow, 1980), p.76.
8. Beacham, *op.cite*, p.7.
9. Paul Jeffery, *The Collegiate Churches of England and Wales*, (London, 2004), p.117.
10. Canon Michael Warner, *A Gazetteer of Works on Cornish Anglican Churches, 1700–2000* (database at Church House, Truro). *Truro Diocesan Kalendar*, (1902), p.169 and (1905), p.162.
11. Handwritten manuscript by Revd G.M. Parsons, dated 29 November 1907: property of Crantock Church (hereafter *Parsons MSS*). Part of a letter addressed to visitors to the church by Father George Metford Parsons, 1907, reads 'The stained glass … forms a connected scheme, carried out under the Vicar's direction.'
12. *Idem*. The letter continues 'The stained glass in the church is all new, by Mr C.E. Tute of Chipperfield, King's Langley, and Messrs. E.&C. O'Neill, Gray's Inn Road, London WC.' Tute gained his initial experience in the prestigious and popular studio of Charles Eamer Kempe (1837–1907).
13. CRO AD772/488 from letter by Revd G.F. Rickard (his father was a churchwarden of Crantock church).
14. Sedding, *Norman Architecture*, p.71. 'The old collegiate church is therefore redeemed and put right again in the sight of those who reverence God's sanctuary.'
15. Built 1865–70, architect William White, a partial scheme, see www.cornishstainedglass.org.uk – Michael G Swift Maryfield stained glass.
16. Michael G. Swift *The windows of Truro Cathedral – a Victorian vision fulfilled*, Chapter 3, Available on www.cornishstainedglass.org.uk
17. Nicholas Orme, *The Victoria County History of Cornwall, vol. 2, Religious History to 1560*, (London, 2010), p.177.
18. *Parsons M/S and Cornwall County Records* AD772/183.
19. Michael G. Swift, 'Types' are events from the Old testament prefiguring Gospel narratives, used extensively in Bishop Benson's master Scheme for the stained glass windows in Truro Cathedral's sanctuary and baptistry: Michael G. Swift, Chapters 7–9.
20. John Hall *Dictionary of subjects and symbols in Art* (London, 1996), p. 326.
21. Sedding *Norman Architecture*, p.69.
22. Nicholas Orme *Cornwall and the Cross*, (Chichester, 2007), p18. G.H. Doble. *S. Carantoc, Bishop and Confessor*, Cornish Saints, no. 14, 2nd ed. (1932). Nicholas Orme *The Saints of Cornwall*, (Oxford, 2000), pp. 83–5.
23. Nicholas Orme (ed.), *Nicholas Roscarrock's Lives of the Saints: Cornwall and Devon*, (Exeter, 1992), pp.63–4.
24. St Alban's Holborn was built by George Butterfield in the style of his earlier All Saint's, Margaret Street, and both churches were centres for High Church Ritualism in central London.
25. Joseph Clayton, *Father Stanton of St Alban's Holborn*, (London, 1913), chapter 3.
26. Peter Anson *The Call of the Cloister*, (London, 1964).
27. E.W. Benson *The English Cathedral*, (London, 1878), p.159. His intention to name the canons stalls at Truro cathedral after the Cornish saints was 'to read into our own past, and of our connection with the other ancient churches prior to the Romish usurpations'.
28. Swift, www.cornishstainedglass.org.uk chapter 3.
29. *Ibid*, chapter 8.
30. *Truro Diocesan Kalendar*, (1902), p.169, (30th November 1901).
31. *Crantock Parish letter*, (Easter, 1901). 'Cost of North Transept window £80 (glass cost £55) and each of the four nave windows £37.' See Swift, www.cornishstainedglass.org.uk chapter 14.
32. In 1912, the tower appeal received a donation from King George V.
33. Sedding, *Norman Architecture*, p.71.

George Wightwick (1802–72) 'an architect of much ability and a man of exquisite taste'

Rosamund Reid

I am now a very failing elderly gentleman of forty-eight, with little more than my experience for my pains, and that a painful experience; for it has left me to learn that the confidence reposed in the unpracticed youth may be withheld from the veteran: that the hopes once entertained of influence as an Instructor, and of the love of the instructed, have greatly – if not entirely – failed: that efforts at the improvement of public taste and feeling and critical perception, have merely tended to occasional public entertainment; - that I have amused for the hour where I vainly hoped to inform for the day; that devotion to my subject has been unaccompanied by power to advance it; that my imagined mission has proved a mission only imagined, that I have failed to keep the ground which I fondly fancied was entrusted to me; and that in consequence of my inadequacy 'fools (still) rush in where angels fear to tread.'[1]

These self-deprecating comments suggest that George Wightwick saw himself as a man lacking in self-confidence and conviction. This chapter will show that nothing could be further from the truth. He was undoubtedly a successful architect but, as we shall explore, was also a deeply complex, popular and flamboyant man whose absurdity and wit made him equally competent in acting, lecturing and writing. One contemporary fittingly described him as a brilliant and amusing man, something of an eccentric, a man without egoism and conceit, but one whose presence dominated, one in fact who would 'stalk the streets, rather than walk them'.[2]

He was, according to Howard Colvin, 'probably ... the first English architectural journalist'.[3] His extensive writing output however took him far beyond the world of architecture, regularly laying bare in print his varied theoretical views and prejudices on a wide range of topics. Whilst in retirement in Bristol he took great pains to secure his legacy by collecting together many of his professional papers, architectural drawings and watercolor paintings and by writing a comprehensive account of his life that was published in parts for *Bentley's Magazine*.[4] On his death he left his archive to the Royal Institute of British Architects (RIBA).

George Wightwick was born in 1802 in Mold, a small town on the river Alyn in Flintshire. He moved from London to Plymouth in 1827, and retired twenty four years later, having accumulated significant wealth. His father was a country gentleman, and his mother the daughter of the portrait painter, George Taylor. He was an only child and became fatherless when his father accidentally drowned in a canal. His memoirs record the events as he remembered them, and suggests that from an early age he had an interest in architecture — about the tragic night he wrote 'My mother, that night, sat with only her nine year old boy, drawing the outline of a parish church on the slate, which should perhaps have been covered with figures of a multiplication sum for school next morning'.[5]

After the death of his father, Wightwick and his mother moved to London, and it was four years later his mother married again, this time to William Damant, a member of the Stock Exchange and a widower with two children. It was Damant's daughter whom Wightwick was to marry later when Damant had retired from business and the family had moved to Yelverton in Devon. Once in London Wightwick was articled to the competent, yet conventional, architect and civil engineer, Edward Lapidge, and having completed his training Wightwick spent some months travelling Europe before he set about finding work.

In 1826 he was employed by Sir John Soane as companion and amenuensis, but it was a bitter-sweet association that lasted for only eight months. Soane, professionally established and idiosyncratic as he was, became demanding and irascible, as Wightwick became more and more temperamental and petulant – but out of it came a friendship that lasted until Soane's death in 1837. Wightwick later modelled some of his own practice on Soane's, using his pupils to make meticulous copies of his working drawings, many of which survive within the collections of the RIBA. Soane allowed him to use his name as dedication, first in the maiden issue of Wightwick's *New Western Periodical* (1834) and again, in his publication *A Selection from the museum of the Vatican consisting of Antique Vases, Altars, Chairs and various Architectural Fragments* (1837).[6]

After he left Soane's employ Wightwick was unable to find work in London, and rejoined his family in the west-country. From here he quickly established himself in partnership with John Foulston, a London architect who had settled in Plymouth in 1828 when he was commissioned to design a group of public buildings including the assembly rooms, a hotel and theatre. The partnership came about towards the end of Foulston's career and only lasted a few months before his retirement; however, the bond between the two men was enough for Wightwick to inherit the goodwill of the practice and its outstanding commissions.

Wightwick never achieved national recognition. However he certainly became one of the leading west-country architects of his time, his work, like Foulston's, being essentially eclectic, deploying classical, gothic and Italianate styles with ease. However, his work cannot be dissociated from the time in which he lived, or from that part of the country where he worked, nor in fact from the requests of his patrons. From his membership of the Plymouth Athenaeum, the scientific and cultural institution to which all men of letters in the area belonged, came introductions to the network that led him into Cornwall.

In 1838 one of Wightwick's first major commissions was to augment Foulston's work at the Cornish County Lunatic Asylum at Bodmin. In *Bentley's Miscellany* he

Fig. 1
The Humphrey Gryll's Monument in Helston. Paid for by public subscription in memory of the local philanthropist. Author.

wrote '…my too rapid success was enough to give my brain a twist, which perhaps it did, at least to the extent of delusion, that I was a fair measure *deserving* of that favour'.[7] He began with a wedge shaped addition to the main asylum building, and ended ten years later with a separate new building opened in 1848, as well as designing the superintendent's house. This important and continuing commission introduced him to local patrons who not only gave him work but included him in their social functions. He accepted invitations to speak on architectural matters, as well as on broader issues to do with art and taste, at literary institutes throughout the county. His wish to educate and his manner of speaking made him popular on the lecture circuit. Furthermore his friendship with William Hicks, Domestic Superintendent of the Asylum, led him into many country houses, 'comic book in hand', where the two men were invited to sing and tell stories together, much to Wightwick's delight. He describes these events in some detail in his diary, where he also gives an account of his meetings with asylum patients that is both humorous and touching.[8] It was Sabine Baring-Gould who stated that 'Wightwick had the merit of discovering Hicks and of introducing him to notables in Devon and Cornwall, for, miserable architect though he was, he had got the ear of the public in the west as a man of charming manners and teeming with anecdote'.[9]

Wightwick was led to Helston early on in his west-country career through a friendship with the second son of the poet Samuel Taylor Coleridge, Derwent Coleridge, who was headmaster of the local grammar school and member of the Plymouth Athenaeum. Coleridge became an important client and patron for Wightwick, commissioning a design for a new grammar school and spreading the architect's reputation amongst his peers which resulted in a commission for a new house in 1840 from Frederick Lobb Hill, solicitor and later Town Clerk for Helston, and a monumental arch in memory of the local philanthropist Humphrey Millett Grylls (Fig.1).[10]

Wightwick's appointment for this monument resulted from an open competition, which became controversial because it was decided by just one vote, and that, unsurprisingly, was the vote of his friend Coleridge. It was only after he had advised his friend to modify his design to the requirements and tastes of other members of the committee, warning him of their criticisms, that Wightwick made the necessary changes. This arch, standing at the bottom of Coinagehall Street, is described in *Cornwall* as 'A hefty

Fig. 2
Trrevarno, a classically inspired country house near Sithney, built for Christopher Popham. Author.

Gothic design worthy of its position'.[11] Its bold design draws attention to its *raison d'être* which was not only to celebrate the life of an important magistrate and public benefactor, but also to give testament to the friendship between Coleridge and Wightwick. The inscription reads 'Be it also a monument of grateful Friendship, borne by the Architect, Geo: Wightwick to the Revd. Derwent Coleridge, who, in this, as in many other instances, has been the chief promoter of opportunity for exercising his humble acquirements in Design'.

Through his work at Helston Wightwick went on to design Trevarno, a classically inspired country house near Sithney, for a past High Sheriff of Cornwall, Christopher Popham. (Fig.2). Set within its own lovely gardens, the interiors are finely decorated with delicately moulded cornices, intricately designed ceiling roses, and a curved flying staircase with ornate ironwork. The house was extended in 1874 by the fuse manufacturer and later Member of Parliament William Bickford Smith

Coleridge further introduced Wightwick to Robert Were Fox, the Quaker scientist and philanthropist, who described Wightwick's lecture on 'The Romance of Architecture' as 'the most brilliant lecture I have ever heard'. His brother, Barclay Fox, described Wightwick as 'beautifully ugly – a man who carries the confidence of genius in every tone and action'.[12] Out of this connection came the invitation in 1840 to re-front and alter the Royal Cornwall Philosophical Society's building in Falmouth. Again Wightwick's architectural dexterity is on display with its assertive Greek revival style façade and heavy fluted Doric columns.

In 1840 he designed St John's church (Fig.3) and village complex at Treslothan, near Camborne, for Edward William Pendarves, merchant banker, Justice of the Peace and Member of Parliament for Cornwall and later West Cornwall between 1826 and 1853. The Pendarves family were good friends of the Aclands, who had themselves commis-

Fig. 3 This page *St John's church, Treslothan, built for the Pendarves family as a chapel to Pendarves House. It was this building that destroyed Wightwick's reputation as a church builder.* Author.

Fig. 4 Opposite page, top *St Peter's, Flushing. Exterior. Described in the latest Cornwall (p.198) as 'Romanesque on an aisleless plan with a chancel apse'.* Author.

Fig. 5 Oposite page, below *St Peter's, Flushing. Interior.* Author.

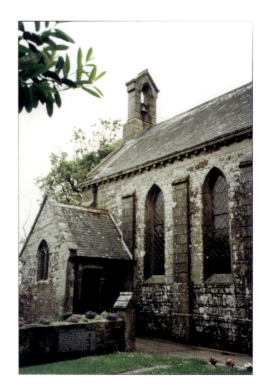

sioned Wightwick to design the church of St Michael and All Angels at Bude alongside other work for the family in north Cornwall. Treslothan is centered on a small green, and incorporated houses for the curate, sexton and schoolmaster, as well as a school and the church, all executed in a Tudor Gothic style. Pendarves and his wife were considered by Wightwick as prominent friends of some years standing until he lost their good opinion when he was blamed for faulty work and a want of vigilance. His employer had been gravely annoyed and his lady 'furious'.[13] If this was not enough, his church design itself was severely criticised, the lack of chancel especially remarked, and even the roof trusses were a cause of censure. The *Ecclesiologist*, the powerful mouthpiece of the Cambridge Camden Society, noted

> This is one of those cases where no mercy ought to be shown to the architect, who, with unlimited funds at his command, has shown that his signal failure is owing to nothing but his own insufficient acquaintance with the art that he professes… The roof resembles that of a railway station…and the lancets…are about as large in proportion to the size of the windows at King's College Chapel.[14]

It was this particular building that finally destroyed his reputation as a church architect.

Wightwick's church work represented Low Church Liberalism, and from this position he would not budge – he refused to cut his coat according to his cloth, and stood by every principle in which he believed. He was of the opinion that a church was for the people, for their comfort and to meet their spiritual needs. A church for him was not about ritual, doctrinal principles and the promotion of faith through the spiritual control of the congregation by the clergy. His church design was of a different order. Wightwick designed nine churches in Devon and Cornwall, of which eight were built, but all more or less criticised by the Ecclesiologists. These churches, like St Peter's, Flushing, with its charming Morris & Co window (later addition) (Figs. 4 and 5), mostly incorporated his beliefs in the box-like shape, with foreshortened chancel, and with no pillars which could obstruct a view of the preacher. Thus the clergy could not distance themselves from the congregation, the pulpit taking precedence over the altar. In the end he was designing churches only for the Evangelicals who, according to Wightwick, required 'church room, and cared not a whit in what form it might be afforded'.

The Molesworth St Aubyn family employed Wightwick to Palladianise, extend and render the east elevation of their 18th century country house at Pencarrow and within the house he designed a shrine for the statue of Aphrodite (Fig.6).[15] Inspired by classical influences he built Penquite, near Golant, a plain spacious house with pediment, and the Italianate style clock tower in Fore Street, Bodmin, commissioned in 1844 by Captain Collins of Trewardale during the mayoralty of his nephew. Towards the end of his career he worked in the prevailing Tudor Gothic style, examples being numerous parsonage houses throughout Cornwall, the parsonage house and school at Pelynt and Luxstowe House, in Liskeard, a substantial and quite imposing house built for William Glencross, the Plymouth builder.

One of his last commissions in Cornwall was also his most prestigious, Tregrehan House at St Blazey for Colonel Edward Carlyon (Fig.7). Onto the original double pile house which dates to c.1680 Wightwick was asked to add a large classical block with a colonnade of paired Ionic columns, a portico and porch. In doing so the interiors were reordered, a grand staircase added and the 18th century high roof of the original building replaced with a lower hipped roof. During this work he designed a pair of book presses, one of which still survives in the house.

Wightwick's world was broad, and was not confined to his buildings alone. Out of his own painful experience in dealing with his patrons (and most particularly with their wives) he wrote his terms of employment and published them in the *Architect*.[16] He wrote plays and articles and contributed extensively to journals and newspapers all his life.[17] In John Weale's *Quarterly Papers on Architecture* (1844) he expressed his own religious principles which

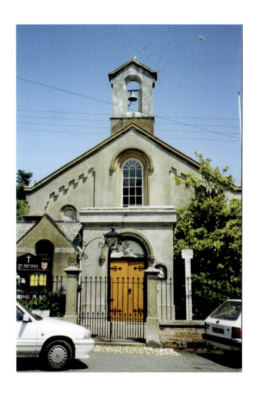

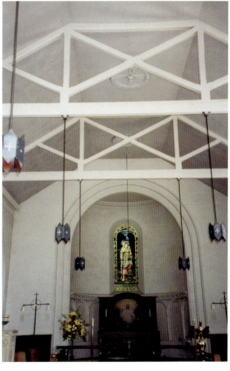

were so much at variance with those of the Camden Society. In retirement he wrote extensively under the pseudonym of Roderick Ramble for local newspapers – his writings covered a wide array of topics ranging from architecture, art and politics to social issues. Many of these articles are very humorous – of William Butterfield's church of All Saints, Margaret Street, London, he spoke with scorn describing it as a building that a brick-maker might construct to show off his varied stock in trade. On another occasion he advocated quite passionately that every domestic servant should be allowed adequate time for church attendance. He collated many of these articles into cuttings books which are still held in the local libraries of Bristol and Plymouth. His published books are beautifully produced but are now quite difficult to find. Perhaps his most significant work remains *The Palace of Architecture: a Romance of Art and History* (1840) which particularly represents his eclectic architectural style and his quirkiness. His dedication to Frances, Countess of Morley, declares 'My object, in this Work, is to promote just appreciation in Architecture, in the minds of all who are susceptible of the Beautiful, the Poetical, and the Romantic. Should I be fortunate to merit YOUR suffrage, I shall have the better hope of securing theirs.'[18]

George Wightwick was a visionary and a dreamer. At times he comes across at odds with the world in which he lived. That he enhanced west-country life there can be no doubt. His anecdotes proliferate in the pages of local literature and contemporary newspapers; it is perhaps significant that he wrote obituaries of many of his contemporaries. Those he met did not easily forget him. Alfred, Lord Tennyson, remembered travelling from Plymouth to Tavistock with Wightwick in 1848, recalling the meeting

Fig. 6
Pencarrow House near Bodmin. Wightwick designed a shrine for the statue of Aphrodite in the music room adjoining the front hall. Author.

Fig. 7 *Tregrehan House, St Blazey. A 17th century house extended first, by William Wood of Truro in the 18th century and second, by Wightwick in the 19th. Around the same time William Eden Nesfield redesigned the garden and park.* Author.

'…in the most minutest circumstance, even to the cabman's rowing us for smoking in his cab'.[19] When the architect died the *Western Daily Mercury* reported that he was 'a kind, warm-hearted, genial man … an architect of much ability and a man of exquisite taste'.[20]

This chapter has recalled not only Wightwick's architectural contribution to the south west but also his other impacts on the cultural world in which he lived. Perhaps his complexity is well summed up by the last words in his book *The Palace of Architecture*, where he wrote 'And – nothing now remains – but one sad word – "Farewell!"'[21] Disengaging with his reader was difficult and tortuous, a situation he compares to 'Imogen in parting with Posthumous'. As he '…beg[s] to tender our parting of affectionate respect' he concludes

> Whatever our 'madness' in *castle-building*, she may still acknowledge there is some 'method in it;' she may, at all events, generously confess the cost at which we have constructed this manifold Monument of our Folly, and kindly lament the fruitless issue of many a toilsome day and sleepless night.[22]

Notes

1. RIBA WiG/1/1. Introduction to a bound copy of Wightwick's hand-written lectures to the Athenaeum, delivered from 8 January, 1828. The lectures are entitled 'Patriarchal, Egyptian, Grecian and Roman architecture'; 'Christian architecture'; 'Hindu, Mahomedan and other styles of architecture'; 'Architecture poetically considered'; 'Architectural practice' and 'British cathedrals' (in two parts).
2. W.F. Collier, 'Some Sixty Years Reminiscences of Plymouth', *Report and Transactions of the Devonshire Association for the Advancement of Science, Literature and Art*, (July, 1892), vol.xxiv, p.93.
3. Howard Colvin, *A Biographical Dictionary of British Architects 1600–1840*, (Newhaven and London, 1995), p.1050.
4. George Wightwick, 'Life of an Architect', *Bentley's Miscellany*, vols. 31–5 and 42–3, (1852–4 and 1857–8).
5. *Ibid.*, vol.31, (1852), p.326.
6. George Wightwick, *A selection from the museum of the Vatican: consisting of antique vases, altars, chairs, and various architectural fragments* (London, 1837).
7. Wightwick, *Life*, vol.42, (1857), p.403.
8. RIBA WiG/1/2, p.157.
9. S. Baring-Gould, *Cornish Characters and Strange* Events, (London, 1908), p.510
10. Grylls was much mourned as landowner, mining magnate, public benefactor, magistrate and elected Mayor of Helston four times between 1817 and 1832.
11. Pevsner (2014), p.246.
12. R.L. Brett (Ed.), *Barclay Fox's Journal*, (London, 1979). p.105
13. Wightwick, *Life*, p.157
14. Anon, 'New Churches', *The Ecclesiologist*, New Series, vol.1, (July, 1845), p.185.
15. Paul Holden, 'Cornish Classicism: Pencarrow, Cornwall. The Home of the Molesworth-St Aubyn family', *Country Life*, vol. 204, no. 31, (4 August 2010), pp.46–51.
16. *The Architect*, ii, (1850), p.28.
17. He contributed to the Critic between 1852 and 1858, discussing individual buildings as well as the state of the architectural profession.
18. George Wightwick, *The Palace of Architecture*, (London, 1840), n.p.
19. C.Y. Lang and E.F. Shannon (Eds.), *Letters of Alfred, Lord Tennyson*. (Oxford, 1987), vol. II, p,189, letter dated November 1857
20. *Western Daily Mercury*, 13 August 1872

A Cornish Connoisseur and Builder: Lieutenant-Colonel Charles Lygon Cocks (1821–85)

Jeremy Pearson

Between 1858 and 1864, fresh from serving in the Crimean War and still an officer in the Coldstream Guards, Charles Cocks built a small Tudor Gothic manor for himself near Liskeard in the parish of St Neot. Although Treverbyn Vean has been attributed jointly to George Gilbert Scott and Henry Rice of Liskeard with some interiors by William Burges, there is little doubt that Cocks took a presiding and eager interest in the project himself, perhaps even having a commanding hand in the design. This chapter will explore the building schemes of Colonel Cocks, a man who epitomised the ambitions of the socially aspiring mid-Victorian gentleman-soldier. It will also assess his role as a notable collector, connoisseur and amateur photographer. We are fortunate that his inscribed photograph album with 462 images taken during the 1860s and 1870s survives, it being a valuable record not only of his own Cornish home but also the homes of his family, friends and neighbours, as well as many other places in England and abroad.[1]

Fig.1 *Colonel Charles Lygon Cocks (1821–85).* National Trust/Lanhydrock

Charles Lygon Cocks (Fig.1) was born in June 1821 at Downing Street, Westminster. He was the third son of the successful banker Thomas Cocks and his wife, Agneta, daughter of the Right Honourable Reginald Pole Carew of Antony in East Cornwall. Her Scandinavian name is indicative of the time her father spent on clandestine government missions in Norway and Sweden looking at mining and other industries. The Cocks family were a long established Worcestershire family, cousins to the Yorkes of Forthampton, near Tewkesbury, one of whom had already married into the Pole Carew family, and it is perhaps through this relationship that

Thomas met his bride. Agneta was related to the Bullers of Morval and the Edgcumbes of Mount Edgcumbe and Charles spent considerable time with both. It is suggestive that his interest in photography came from the pioneer photographer William Henry Fox Talbot of Lacock, who was half-brother to Caroline, Countess of Mount Edgcumbe, and regular visitor to her Cornish home.

Thomas was the head of the Cocks Biddulph bank which enabled him to buy a lavish country seat called Thames-banks at Great Marlow in Buckinghamshire where Charles and his seven brothers and sisters lived and were educated.[2] He was destined for an army career and so went to Sandhurst, later becoming an Ensign (by purchase) in 1838 and two years later a Lieutenant in the Coldstream Guards. Whilst serving in the Middle East and India he had time to pursue artistic interests; some drawings from this period of his life survive in the National Army Museum in Chelsea. His cousin William Cocks of Falmouth was a prominent member of the Penzance Natural History and Antiquarian Society and it was perhaps through this link that he was invited to present a paper to the group entitled 'Notes on the Botany of the Bosphorous and Varna'.[3]

Thanks to the financial backing of his family he rose through the ranks becoming a Lieutenant Colonel in 1855. He served with great distinction at the siege of Sebastopol in 1856 and was awarded the 'medal, with clasp, of the Medjidie and the Turkish medal'. After the defeat of the Russians he returned to this country and spent a consid-

Fig. 2
Treverbyn Vean from the south east. National Trust/Lanhydrock.

erable amount of time at his grandparents' house at Antony. He continued to serve in the Coldstream Guards until 1860, retiring at the age of 39 when he became a popular and respected member of the local community where he served as commander of the East Cornwall Battalion of Volunteers, Justice of the Peace and Deputy Lieutenant for the shire.

Sometime between 1851 and 1858 he purchased a parcel of land to the north of the Liskeard to Bodmin turnpike road and set about creating a home suitable for his status. In the previous two decades a number of his extensive cousinry had completed major building works – the Pole Carews had built a rectory at Maryfield (1847) designed by William White and the 3rd Earl of Mount Edgcumbe had built a fifty room Italianate house called the Winter Villa (1855) overlooking Firestone Bay at Stonehouse, Plymouth. Likewise the Yorkes at Forthampton were talking to the young William Burges about changes to the parish church, and the erection of some Gothic, high gabled almshouses, while another cousin, Earl Somers of Eastnor Castle in Herefordshire, had recently commissioned furniture from A.W.N. Pugin, which was made for him by the firm of J.C. Crace in Wigmore Street in London.

Inspired by such projects Cocks turned to the eminent London-based George Gilbert Scott (1811–78) for his own robust manor house (Fig.2). Scott was working in Cornwall at the time with some new external buildings and an internal restoration of Lanhydrock, near Bodmin, for the Agar-Robartes family and the restoration of the church and the building of a rectory at Kilkhampton near Bude. In addition Scott was employed on building two large country houses (Kelham Hall in Nottinghamshire and Walton Hall in Warwickshire) and the restoration of another (Sudeley Castle in Gloucestershire) so it is perhaps not surprising to see that he turned to Henry Rice of Liskeard (1808–76) to assist. Overseeing these Cornish projects for Scott was his 'chief assistant' or south west agent the Liskeard-born Richard Coad (1825–1900), who had trained with Henry Rice.

Treverbyn Vean is built of local stone, the main front is dominated by two high gables with every facade enlivened by different features – an oriel window, a large two storey bay or a massive chimney stack. The kitchen on the north west side is slightly detached. The interior is described in *Cornwall* as '…a full-height hall with C15–style arch-braced collar-truss roof with wind-braces, a gallery with cusped braces and pierced panels, and a spectacular French Gothic style fireplace with attached columns and a tall tapering hood'.[4] The reception rooms on the south east front display 'panelled ceilings with carved bosses and four-centred doorways with linenfold panelled doors and original door furniture', one such room was delightfully named the 'Bower of Calm Delight'.[5] (Fig.3) For the principal reception room Colonel Cocks commissioned William Burges (1827–81), an emerging architect and designer, to design a mas-

Fig. 3
'The Bower of Calm Delight', Treverbyn Vean. National Trust/Lanhydrock.

sive ornamental plasterwork fireplace depicting the legend of St Neot who had rescued a stag whose antlers had been caught during the chase – by happy coincidence the symbol of the harts antlers was also found on the Colonel's coat of arms. The fireplace was carved by John Birnie Philip, perhaps on the recommendation of Scott.

A contemporary description of Treverbyn Vean and its decoration given by William Lake in his *Parochial History of Cornwall* (1870) seems to confirm that Cocks had had a major hand in the design of his new property

> Treverbyn Vean the interesting country residence of Col. C.L. Cocks was built a few years ago, from the proprietor's own designs in the manor-house style. The dining room is panelled with cedar brought from Bermuda by Admiral Boscawen and the roofs of the entrance hall, with the minstrel's gallery, the Dining and Drawing Rooms were made from the teakwood of the Orinoco

which conveyed Col Cock's Battalion of Coldstreamers out to the East in 1854. On the Drawing Room chimney piece is represented the legendary story of St Neot, which was designed by W. Burges, and shown at the Art Exhibition of 1862.[6]

As mentioned by Lake the drawing room was undoubtedly a highlight of the bachelor Colonel's new house – panelled and hung with tapestry as a fashionable re-creation of a cluttered medieval interior (Fig.4). Within the room was the 'Wheel of Fortune' table, a remarkable piece of furniture, similar to a table that Earl Somers had commissioned only a few years earlier for Eastnor castle.[7] Made by Crace to Burges design, the octagonal table had a marquetry top inlaid with ivory, mother of pearl and metals and sat on a Puginesque oak base; it was displayed at the International Exhibition, London, in 1862.

Cocks also commissioned ironwork and silver from the fashionable firm of 'Medieval Metalworkers' John Hardman and Co of Birmingham, with whom his family had already had several dealings. He might also have seen some of the Hardman's recent exquisite work at the cathedral of St Mary and St Boniface in Plymouth which was constructed between 1856 and 1858 to designs by J. A. and C. F. Hansom. The Hardman archive (now divided between Birmingham Museum and Art Gallery and Birmingham Archives and Heritage) reveals the very close interest in which Cocks took in the design and production and the wide range of 'medieval metalwork' that they supplied. In March 1852 a brass bedstead with 'special springs'(costing £21.12s.6d), a present from his father, was delivered to 'Antonie House, Torpoint, Davenport' (sic).[8] In the same year his eldest brother had given him four silver table salts and a drinking cup, one of his sisters presented him with silver Gothic toast rack and his youngest brother Octavius presented him with a Hardman cream jug designed by Pugin (£6.10s.0d).

The Colonel's first recorded commission was in 1860 when he ordered a large medieval style silver coffee pot, with the arms of the Somers and the Cocks family on either side (£35.0s.0d and its box 1s.6d). When it arrived he was not entirely satisfied with it. Further correspondence and accompanying sketches show that he requested a slightly different design for the body of the jug, the pot was then returned to Hardmans when after a few months, and at a further charge of £7.14s.6d, it was returned to Cornwall and Cocks reported that 'the work is completed very much to my satisfaction'.[9] Some of the Colonel's collection was displayed on the table and dresser in the dining room. (Fig.5)

In 1870 Cocks married Josephine Chichester Nagle (1840–1926),[10] daughter of Joseph Chichester Nagle of Calverleigh Court in mid-Devon and his wife Lady Henrietta, daughter of the 4th Earl of Portsmouth of Eggesford, north Devon.[11] His marriage prompted further commissions which his friends then presented to the happy couple. As an established customer of Hardmans, Colonel Cocks was much involved with the designs for a variety of items which included a silver pepper pot from Lady Elizabeth Villiers, a mustard pot and spoon given by the Hon. Frederick Villiers, a large tapersick paid for by Francis J. Chichester of Crediton, a large salver in the medieval

Opposite
Fig. 4 *The Drawing Room, Treverbyn Vean.*
National Trust/ Lanhydrock

Fig. 5
The Dining Room, Treverbyn Vean. National Trust/ Lanhydrock

style with an enamelled central boss from his sister Charlotte, some sugar tongs with birds claws from Lady Bucknall Estcourt and a teapot presented by Major General H.D. White.[12]

Once Treverbyn Vean was completed Cocks immersed himself into various other occupations. Alongside raising his young family he took up photography with some enthusiasm, travelled widely, particularly to Spain and Malta, and took a great interest in art and architecture. His design skills were also in demand, and he was commissioned to design a tomb chest for Bishop Millman of Calcutta (d. 1876) (Fig.6) and a memorial cross for Lieutenant George Glanville of the Bengal European Fusiliers with whom he had served in his youth.

By an 1876 Act of Parliament a new diocese for Cornwall was created, carved out of the large Diocese of Exeter. The new prelate, Edward Benson, former Headmaster of Wellington College and later Archbishop of Canterbury, was much admired by Queen Victoria as a man of energy and vision. His purpose, as he saw it, was to create a cathedral worthy of the new diocese. Although several large churches in the county were considered as possible cathedrals it was soon determined that a new church should be built in Truro, and that the William, 4th Earl of Mount Edgcumbe, Lord Lieutenant of the county and Provincial Grand Master of the Freemasons, should be chairman of the organising committee. Seeking a man of experience, sensitivity and energy 'Bill' Mount Edgcumbe appointed his friend 'Charlie' Cocks as his deputy chairman. Moving with some speed a limited competition to find an architect was held and John Loughborough Pearson was appointed to build a new cathedral in the French style which, because of its constricted site, would dominate by height rather than size. It was also determined that it should incorporate part of the existing medieval St Mary's parish church which made for later complications.

The adjoining twenty four properties were soon purchased, and demolished, and amidst great ceremony the foundation stone was laid in May 1879. Pearson's plans were accepted by the Building Committee in August of the same year and were subsequently praised by *The Building News* as 'equal to anything that the gifted architect has yet produced and we question if any other living architect would have produced a more suitable and masterly design'.[13]

Fig. 6 *Bishop Millman's tomb, Calcutta.* National Trust/Lanhydrock

But to the huge consternation of the Cornish, the architect proposed that the whole of the building should be constructed of 'the finest Bath stone' which he was currently using at a church in Torquay.[14] The organising committee rapidly determined that the county's cathedral should be built of Cornish stones, a point Pearson reluctantly conceded in May 1881.[15] Along with Pearson's clerk of works, James Bubb, Cocks was commissioned to visit all likely quarries in the county and bring samples back for the committee's consideration. They returned with seventy two samples, from which the choice of Mabe, St Stephens-in-Brannel granites and other stones were made. They also had to gauge the amount of stone which could be supplied, and the transport infrastructures available to deliver them. Ideally the chosen quarry had to be able to produce fifty tons of stone a week, here the Colonel's knowledge of his adopted county and his links to the aristocratic or gentry families who owned many of the quarries proved invaluable and they were able to proceed with speed. Assisted by Arthur Hamble of Looe and Canon Phillpotts of Porthgwidden an interim report was tabled in August and by the end of September a final report presented which suggested the range of stones which could be used. A local paper was glad to report

> The same care is being taken to select the stone as in putting it in place. No less than seventy two varieties of stone have been examined and reported upon, and out of these there were a certain number decided upon, and some idea of the harmonious blending of the various colours of the stone can now be formed. The whole of the external ashlar work is from the granite quarries at Mabe, and the interior ashlar of the softer stone known as St Stephens granite. For the interior a variety of oolite will be used, together with the beautiful sage green from the Earl of Mount Edgcumbe's quarry, the Tarten Down quarry near St Germans and a beautiful pink elvan from the quarries in the neighbourhood of Doublebois known as Lantewy stone.[16]

Cocks took a great interest in the cathedral. He photographed some of the stones for reference and his many letters described features which he had seen and admired elsewhere as well as highlighting concerns from some Cornish families about memorials in the new building, and expressing his own preference for Pentewan stone. As a single-minded man of strong faith he was honoured to be involved in this great project however he never saw its completion.

Cocks died in 1885, aged 69. An obituary in the *Cornish Times* reported 'In that capacity (as deputy Chairman of the organising committee) he visited nearly every important quarry in the county, and reported upon the stones in them in a manner which was astonishing for its exhaustiveness'.[17] His friends and relations knew how close to his heart this great scheme had been and filled the windows of the south wall of the south transept with stained glass by Clayton and Bell in his memory.[18] Perhaps the final words on this remarkable man should be those of his long standing friend the Earl of Mount Edgcumbe who wrote '[Charles Lygon Cocks was] a gallant soldier, a true friend and real Christian – the most tender hearted and kindest of men'.

Following his death Josephine continued to live at Treverbyn Vean, but after her death it was sold. It has subsequently passed through several hands including Lord Beaverbrook's, it was said that Winston Churchill and Field Marshall Montgomery discussed war strategy at the house. Beaverbrook sold the house to his daughter Mrs Janet Kidd in 1947. By now called Pengelly Barton the house was transformed, the Burges fireplace removed in pieces and is buried in the garden along with some stained glass and some of the murals painted over. Today the house is privately owned and divided into three units.

Notes

1. Now in the collections of the National Trust at Lanhydrock.
2. Richard Coad, a Cornish architect working in private practice from Adelphi, London, built the Cocks Biddulph bank in Whitehall between 1870 and 1873 and later extended the Biddulph family home, Ledbury Park, with James M. MacLaren.
3. Published in the *Transactions of the Penzance Natural History and Antiquarian Society*, Vol.II, (1855) p.286.
4. Pevsner (2014), pp.598–9.
5. Idem.
6. William Lake, *A Complete Parochial history of Cornwall*, Vol.3, (Truro, 1870), p.410.

7   Charlotte Gere and Michael Whiteway, *Nineteenth Century Design: from Pugin to Mackintosh* (London 1993), p.211, pl.26.
8   The bed was altered in 1852 with '4 Acorns' and '12 Ornamental Braces' costing £12. More details in Margaret Belcher (ed.), *The Letters of A.M.W. Pugin 1851–1852*, (Oxford, 2015), p.118, note.3.
9   Birmingham Archives and Heritage, correspondence (metalwork) marked C.
10 His wife was 19 years his junior, they had twin daughters in 1873 – Josephine (d.1955) and Honoria (d.1929) neither had issue.
11 J.C. Nagle commissioned George Wightwick to build Calverleigh Court for him in 1844. He was also much involved with the design and construction of St John's (Roman Catholic) church and presbytery in Tiverton built to designs by G.A. Boyce between 1836 and 1839.
12 A full discussion of the silver and other metalwork supplied by Hardman for Treverbyn Vean is given in Martin Levy, 'Some silver by John Hardman & Co for Charles Lygon Cocks', *The Decorative Arts Society Journal*. No.20, (1996), pp.1–10.
13 *Building News*, (1880), p.506 and p.535.
14 Quoted in Anthony Quiney, *John Loughborough Pearson*, (New Haven and London, 1979), p.143.
15 So controversial was the question of stone, the *Western Morning News* refused to publish any more letters on the subject.
16 CRO Truro Cath MSS255/2 (newspaper cutting)
17 *Cornish Times, 23 March 1885.*
18 Michael Swift, https://www.cornishstainedglass.org.uk/mgstc/chapter9.xhtml accessed 27 January 2016.

Goth or Vandal? A re-appraisal of James Piers St Aubyn and Cornwall's Anglican churches.

Michael Warner

For over a century, the architectural output of James Piers St Aubyn (1815–95) has received a significant amount of unfair criticism from professionals and amateurs alike.[1] The focus of such nihilistic comments concerns his church work, particularly his designs, methods of restoration and a perceived iconoclasm to the interior of the buildings that he worked on. This chapter challenges his critics and, in doing so, re-appraises his work in light of current research.[2] Moreover, I will argue that previous assessments of his work have not fully considered two vital influences: first, the difficulties he inherited with the existing condition of Cornwall's Anglican churches and second, the financial climate at the time.

Since his death, St Aubyn's reputation has taken a pounding. In 1912, M.B. Adams wrote

> J.P. St Aubyn was among the first English architects of the gothic revival to recognize the importance of local modes and texture, his church work in Cornwall being studied in this way. It is a matter of regret that he did not retain more of the historical screen work and wood fittings in some of the churches he repaired.[3]

On 4 August 1948 John Betjeman reproached St Aubyn on BBC Radio, he said

> Cornish people will not willingly forgive Mr. J.P. St Aubyn for his workmanlike, but hideous, restoration of most Cornish churches. His signature is iron foot-scraper by the porch (Fig.1). If you see that foot-scraper you know J.P. St Aubyn has been at the church and there will not be much that's old left inside the building.

In 1973 H.M. Brown wrote, '…his work usually left little behind to remind us of ancient days…one cannot enter an over-restored church without a pang for what could have been.'[4] A point repeated in the newly revised edition of *Cornwall*

> …his restorations were unnecessarily destructive: he had a fondness for insert-

ing new and somewhat assertive arch- and wind-braced roofs to replace the simple Cornish waggon roof and for moving features such as tracery and piscinas around between churches. The heavy handed character of a St Aubyn restoration becomes wearisome because of the sheer volume of his work.[5]

Later in the same volume, St Aubyn's un-credited restorations of 1864 and 1873 for Lanteglos-by-Camelford, are noted as being, 'heavy handed… and that left the interior with an unexpectedly austere character', whilst the entry for Mawnan states, 'A drastic restoration in 1880…it bears all the hallmarks of J.P. St Aubyn at his most severe'.[6]

By the early years of the 19th century, the majority of ecclesiastical buildings were in a deplorable state of repair as a direct result of clerical indifference, haphazard administration and carelessness. Such neglect was exacerbated by a significant lack of funds, especially through the gradual cessation of the levying of the Church Rate.[7] A study of the Rural Deans' reports on church fabric between 1807 and 1825[8] and churchwarden's accounts[9] detail the problems, though the observations of Sir Stephen Glynne[10] succinctly note the condition of many of them. At Mabe, for example, he noted that 'the interior presents an appearance of sad neglect, has sad ugly pews. The North side is greatly out of repair, and the wall is strengthened by large ugly buttresses outside and wooden beams within'; at Mevagissey, he saw 'a miserable church in bad repair and altogether dirty and neglected'; at Lanteglos-by-Fowey, he found, 'The church is much neglected and out of repair' and at St Enodoc, 'the whole has a very forlorn and neglected appearance, and the sand has risen so high as to make it easy to ascend the wall and walk between the roofs of the nave and aisle, whence a view of the church is easily obtained through a kind of sky-light.'.[11]

The Anglican Church in Cornwall responded to this situation by restoring and enhancing over 95% of the pre-1800 churches, and building new churches, mission halls and rooms.[12] Within this Victorian building frenzy, St Aubyn was one of a significant number of active participants. The 313 major schemes involved 101 architects, both professional and amateur, who ranged from nationally recognised professionals such as St Aubyn himself (101 schemes), William Butterfield, Richard Coad (3), George Fellowes Prynne (19), James Hine (13), John Loughborough Pearson, E.H. Sedding (38), J.D. Sedding (24), George Edmund Street (8), Silvanus Trevail (6) and William White (12), to talented 'amateurs', amongst whom were the Reverends Ernest Geldart, William Haslam, Francis Hingeston-Randolph (9) and William Willimott, who, as Vicars or Rectors of the parishes themselves, or being acquainted with those who were, restored or designed new buildings, sometimes undertaking the Clerk of Works' role themselves.

Fig 1. *J P St Aubyn's signature foot-scraper, church of St John the Baptist, Penzance.* Author.

The sheer scale of St Aubyn's works shows that he undertook almost three times the number of schemes than E.H. Sedding alone, and more than the total of E.H. and J.D.

Fig.2 *St Stedyana's church, Stithians. North aisle window opening showing the medieval cill and Victorian brickwork arch.* Author.

Fig 3. *South aisle baptistery window at Stithians showing medieval voussoirs and line of additional brickwork.* Author.

Sedding, G.F. Prynne and the firm of Hine and Odgers combined. In reference to the 138 new liturgical buildings, the identified architects and surveyors built eighty of them however, some were awarded more work than others. St Aubyn himself built twenty, more than three times the number of George Wightwick who built six and five times the amount of Charles Hutchens who built four.[13] Whilst there are no documented reasons why he was offered such a substantial number of projects it is pertinent perhaps that he had close family ties with an influential Cornish family.

In general, the scope of restoration and remedial work to be undertaken was dependent upon two things; the existing state of the building and the available budget. The situation that St Aubyn found at St Mary, Callington between 1857 and 1858 is typical; the fabric had been poorly maintained over many years and the interior had been re-ordered to accommodate galleries. The roof slates had completely perished; the flat, aisle roofs substituted with lean-to roofs, thereby blocking up the clerestory windows, whilst the tracery and mullions of the windows were either dreadfully mutilated or entirely destroyed, and replaced with sash windows of poor glass; the battlements needed repairing and the walls re-pointing.

In 1828, at St Cuby, Tregony, to fulfil the requirement to increase free sittings from thirty seats to 290, the medieval roof was discarded and the south arcade removed; the exterior walls were made thinner and higher, a vast simple single pitched roof was

Fig.4 *St Uda, St Tudy, a simple Cornish church with no chancel arch. Restored by St Aubyn between 1872 and 1873 at a cost of £1,151.* Author.

raised and a gallery inserted at the west end. The failure of these works, of poor design and materials, directly contributed to the need for a complete rebuild by the end of the 19th century. In 1866, the Exeter Diocesan Architectural Association observed, 'wooden windows and every symptom of degradation.'[14] Inevitably, the weight of the overall roof caused the failure of the top of the reduced north and south walls, and therefore parishioners of a poor parish had to undertake two major schemes of repair and restoration in seventy years. The second restoration was begun in 1897 after St Aubyn's death, 'the church having been rendered unfit for use by storms';[15] there is a copy of a plan in his hand is in the church vestry.

At a cost of over £1,500, the exterior walls were lowered, and the arcades and two roofs were re-instated, however, the tower remained un-restored,[16] with this work not being undertaken until 1915, a typical example of an incomplete Victorian restoration through lack of funds. The brief entry from the *Truro Kalendar* does not add the details concerning provision of the second-hand seating, some having come from Gulval parish church, restored by St Aubyn in 1891, and with further seating acquired during the on-going restoration of the neighbouring parish church of Creed in 1904, again to St Aubyn's designs.

At Stithians, St Aubyn commenced a programme of re-building and restoration in 1862, part of which entailed the provision of plasterwork up to 15 cms thick to level the profile of the leaning north aisle arcade. This plasterwork failed in 1984, and subsequently all the interior plaster was removed in 1985,[17] revealing the condition of the church before the St Aubyn restoration, and the work that was undertaken. In a north aisle window (Fig.2), the medieval voussoirs had been removed when the sash win-

Fig.5. *St John the Baptist, Penzance. South-east corner. A chapel, showing the decorative Doulting stone details and the stairs leading to the meeting rooms in the crypt.* Author.

dows were installed in the 18th century, leaving the medieval cill in situ, with a complete brick window arch having to be inserted by St Aubyn. The south aisle (Fig.3) baptistery window still retained the medieval voussoirs, whilst St Aubyn used a line of brickwork to build up the exterior of the window-opening after the square-headed sash windows had been removed. It can be assumed that the costs relating to the installation of new Polyphant stone mullions and tracery in all of the windows, together with new roofs over this three-aisled church, had consumed so much of the available funds that the cheapest scissor-truss design of the roof timbers were specified, and instead of correcting the lean of the north arcade by re-building, St Aubyn specified the plasterwork to make the finish vertical.[18]

At Perranarworthal, a wealthier neighbouring parish to Stithians, St Aubyn installed a fine, arch-braced roof between 1880 and 1881, as part of a virtual re-build of the existing church, costing £1,293,[19] though the parish could afford neither pews nor an organ, both of which were installed in 1902.[20]

An understanding of the budgetary constraints upon St Aubyn's schemes can be deduced from the fact that the decades of the 1860s and 1870s, when he began the majority of his schemes, were a time of the collapse of the mining industry. The population of St Just-in-Penwith, where he restored the church in 1866, fell from 9,000 to 6,400 during the 1860s, and at Gwennap, where the restoration started in 1862 and took twenty nine years, the population fell from 11,000 to 6,000 between 1841 and 1881.[21] Church of England clergy, churchwardens and congregations were trying to restore in a financial depression, and this allied to the growth of Non-Conformist congregations, had a detrimental effect on the availability of funds.

Occasionally, there were artistic and design conflicts, as well as concerns over financial costs, and at Gwennap, St Aubyn were involved in a particular conflict over pews and seating. In 1878, the *West Briton* newspaper carried a lengthy article on the re-opening of the church after substantial restoration, noting,

> ...but to such lengths have the dissentions been carried that the architect, Mr J Piers St Aubyn, than whom there are few more trustworthy authorities on church architecture, was discharged by the committee, because he disapproved of half the seats being supplied with doors, and the other half being left open....It is unfortunately, much to be feared that the Bishop will be called upon to decide the questions of appropriated or un-appropriated seats.[22]

The restoration of this large and lofty church took nearly thirty years, a time span that meant that items previously repaired and restored needed further work, with the west end being recorded as 'thoroughly repaired, in 1892'.[23]

When the subjective and simplistic criticism of St Aubyn has been made, the existing condition of the buildings has been ignored, as has the limitation of the funds available. This criticism can be challenged, and a wider disciplined view is taken of his work, though a question may fairly be posed, 'Is it considered that the buildings paid too high an aesthetic price after St Aubyn worked on them, in that too much was swept away?' It is unlikely that the restorers generally, and St Aubyn in particular, deliberately set out to strip the churches however, an awareness of the existing condition of the buildings is vital. Anglican clergy and parishioners, with a declining fabric around them, saw Non-Conformists meeting for worship in new buildings, often with school rooms and ancillary facilities, including toilets, and so eagerly embarked on the challenging opportunity to 'modernise' their building and its contents. They were re-examining the way they conducted the services, modernising the heating, the lighting, creating new hymn books, purchasing new furnishings, commissioning skilled craftspeople to provide new coloured glass in the windows, new woodwork and stonework, using new fabrics and installing new harmoniums and organs; the list of improvements is virtually endless.

The recognition that St Aubyn reported the stonework at Callington had decayed, and it is highly likely that the mullions there were also mutilated because of the sash windows, is typical. Evidence of such stonework can be seen at Duloe parish church, where fragments of old, worked masonry line the path, and at Stithians where part of a Victorian 'new' wall to a churchyard extension was made from discarded broken worked stone and window mullions. It was easier, and cheaper, to create new mullions than to try and put together stonework that had been broken and adapted over hundreds of years as the windows were broken out and sash, or multi-paned, windows installed.

St Aubyn is criticised for his severity, however we do not have an insight into the mind-set, liturgical attitudes and the discussions of the St Aubyn family at Clowance, their ancestral home, as they were considering, for example, the restoration of their parish church of Crowan; nor are we worshipping in a decaying and potentially dangerous building. The concept of 'conservation' in the frenzy of mid-Victorian church restoration was alien, and indeed if items were considered to be 'conserved', the expertise, skills, and especially the funds, were not easily available.

Fig 6. *St John the Baptist. Penzance. J.P. St Aubyn's largest complete church in Cornwall, Built on a challenging site between 1880 and 1881 the church cost £6,130 to complete. The fabric consisted of local Castle-an-Dinas stone with Ham Hill stone detailing.* Author.

St Aubyn designed and built significant new churches at Penzance, St John; Marazion; and St John's-in-the-fields, Halsetown; Treleigh and Penponds, with some on challenging sites, such as Gunnislake and Hessenford; and the smaller mission churches of Trythall and Bridgend. He created sympathetic and beautifully designed interiors that can be seen at Perranuthnoe, Gwennap and St Tudy (Fig.4); the chancels at St Issey and Calstock, the marble reredos at Tuckingmill and the porch and organ loft at Treslothan. His restoration achievements of nearly a third of Cornwall's medieval churches should be celebrated, work he undertook within the budgets available and with fundraising a constant background task. If this had not happened, then simply we would not have the opportunity of using them for their original purpose, and studying them today. James Piers St Aubyn merits a higher place than he has hitherto held in the pantheon of Victorian architects working in Cornwall.

Notes

1. St Aubyn was born at Powick Vicarage and died at Marazion, he is buried on St Michael's Mount.
2. M.J.W. Warner, *Gazetteer of works to, and within, Cornish Anglican Churches 1700–2000 (with some earlier events noted)* Unpublished manuscript. The gazetteer lists, from both published and manuscript sources, all of the recorded identifiable works undertaken on the buildings from the mid-18th century to 2000 (with some earlier references), additions and artefacts installed in or to the buildings, dates for the building of new churches and/or restorations, and, where noted, the architects and surveyors, artists and makers, builders and tradespeople responsible for the works. The building's designation, together with published references and the whereabouts of plans, specifications, photographs, drawings and engravings are noted.
3. Maurice B. Adams, 'Architects from George IV to George VI'. *Journal of the Royal Institute of British Architects*, XIX, (29 June 1912), p.607.
4. H.M. Brown. *What to look for in Cornish Churches* (Newton Abbot, 1973), p.51.
5. Pevsner (2014), p.76.
6. *Ibid*. p.281 and 346.
7. H.M. Brown. *The Catholic revival in Cornish Anglicanism*. (St Winnow, 1990), p73 notes that this was a gradual process '…following mounting resistance by Dissenters and others, for example, St Mary's Truro did not collect it after 1858'. The rate was finally abolished by the Parliamentary Act *Abolition of Compulsory Church Rate*, 31, 32 Vict 1868.
8. CRO/AD/59/74.
9. CRO/P/15/5/1.
10. Flintshire Record Office/SG. T. Cann Hughes (ed), 'Sir Stephen Glynne's Notes on the Churches of Cornwall', *Notes and Queries*, vol. CLXVII, (1935), pp.437–9. Sir Stephen Glynne (1807–74) inspected and made architectural notes on 5,530 churches nation-wide. He visited 106 Cornish churches between 1849 and 1870.
11. *Ibid*. Entries for 18 February 1858, 1 February 1853, n.d. 1842 and 2 February 1850 respectively.
12. Rebuilding, the re-ordering of the interior, replacing that which already existed and upgrading; indeed any combination of these. A further problem that can also be identified is that it is often believed that buildings were restored on a certain date; that they only had one restoration. It is true that some had one restoration; however, in a significant number of cases it was the norm for buildings to be gradually restored, often by different architects or surveyors.
13. So prolific was St Aubyn's output that he built more new churches that E.H. Sedding, William White, Silvanus Trevail, John Hayward, J.A. Reeve (3), Hine and Odgers and G.E. Street (2) combined.
14. Exeter Diocesan Architectural Association paper 29, (1866), reporting on the south aisle.
15. Licence for use of church room for divine service recorded in *Truro Kalendar*, (1897), p.154.
16. *Ibid*. (1899), p.162.
17. *Truro Diocesan Faculty Book*, 8, faculty 23/84.
18. The failure of this plaster in 1984 triggered a restoration programme conducted during the incumbency of the author.
19. *Truro Kalendar*. (1882), p.154.
20. *Truro Diocesan Faculty Book*, 2, faculty dated 2 June 1902, p.371.
21. F.E. Halliday *A History of Cornwall* (London, 1975), p.298.
22. *West Briton*, 21 February 1878.
23. *Truro Kalendar*, (1892), p.170. It could be also noted that the west end again needed repairs during the time that the author was incumbent of the parish of Stithians, Perranarworthal and Gwennap, 1983–93.

East Cornwall Churches: does lightning strike twice?

Simon Crosbie

'Architecturally not specially (sic) interesting' wrote a candid Nikolaus Pevsner about St Odulph's church in Pillaton, east Cornwall.[1] More flattering is Peter Beacham's entry in his revised volume of *Cornwall* when he describes the '…splendidly strong' west tower as being 'of very regular granite blocks, C15, of three stages on a high plinth with buttresses set back from the angles, embattled parapet and pinnacles'.[2] On 21 January 2013 the strength of this late-medieval, Grade 1 listed, church was tested to its limits when a bolt of lightning struck the tower causing critical damage to the north-west pinnacle and the severe destabilisation of its north-eastern neighbour. The *Western Morning News* reported 'One of the four pinnacles on the roof, which weigh several

Fig. 1
St Odulph's church in Pillaton, east Cornwall, remnants of falling masonry on the church roof.
Author.

Fig. 2
St Kayna's church at St. Keyne, near Liskeard, hole in roof after masonry fall. Author.

tonnes, has exploded and the main part of it made a huge gaping hole in the body of the main church' (Fig.1).[3]

Amazingly, almost a year to the day, a similar event occurred only eight miles away in the village of St. Keyne, near Liskeard. On 7 January 2014 lightning struck the Grade 2★ listed, 15th-century church dedicated to St Kayna. Once again the north tower pinnacles took the main force of the strike but, unlike at St Odulph's, the lightning earthed, not through an external metal conductor as would be the obvious and predictable route, but within the core of the wall against a modern steel tie that had been inserted during an earlier refurbishment in 2006. The damage inflicted on the church was similar to that at St Odulph's; the north-east pinnacle was blown apart while the one on the south east side was shaken loose. The local media reported the churchwarden's comments 'The first thing I saw was that the spire on top of one of the pinnacles was missing…when I went inside I saw two large holes and two smaller ones in the north aisle roof, caused by falling stone. There was debris everywhere' (Fig.2).[4] This chapter will discuss these comparable incidents and the consequential restoration works that reconstructed both church towers.

At Pillaton the colossal damage caused to the church was in part due to its lack of lightning protection –its solitary provision being a strike rod with down tape was

installed to the south side. It would appear that as the lightning discharged so the energy was drawn towards the Victorian wrought-iron cramps which then super-heated the lime mortar creating first, moisture deep within the stone coursing, and then steam.

This steam, in turn, caused an explosion within the coursed granite throwing the north-west pinnacle into the air. As the stone fell (in blocks up to ½ tonne in weight) it crashed into the lead-covered tower roof thereby ripping the roof coverings, snapping a series of 25mm (1 inch) thick oak boards and the 152mm (6 inches) oak joists below (Fig.3). Several of the larger stones hurtled past the tower parapet, one bounced off of the slate-covered slopes before landing on the main roof valley below. Two large pieces of masonry were thrown a greater distance, tearing through the north aisle roof and destroying

Fig. 3
Damage to the historic fabric at Pillaton. Author.

Fig. 4
Plaster boss, recovered and re-sited in the nave at Pillaton. Author..

Fig. 5
Two church pinnacles at Pillaton after completed restoration programme. Author.

three medieval and Victorian trusses and severely damaging further infrastructure close by. These stones smashed pews below before landing in the south aisle, where one wedged itself up against the porch door jamming it closed. Fortunately the three 18th century, London style, classical memorials to the Tillie family of Pentillie Castle, near St Mellion, in the south transept were unharmed.[5]

Such was the force of the strike that stones were found as far away as a field to the north of the church, as well as being embedded deep within the Cornish hedge and strewn across the tables and chairs of the nearby public house. Upon closer inspection it was evident that the north-east pinnacle had cracked mortar bedding which, after checking with a plumb line, drew us to the conclusion that stones from the north-west pinnacle had hit its neighbour with some considerable force. This, in turn, shifted the granite against its base so that the entire set of stones had become destabilised.

The Ecclesiastical Insurance Company responsible for the building immediately commissioned a team to carry out an initial survey. Once the full impact was understood dialogue with English Heritage established a series of protocols and philosophies for repairs. Unusually, the urgency to stabilise and make safe the damage led to an urgent works programme starting ahead of any Diocese Committee sitting to approve

methods and materials. To facilitate the work (and to provide consistent working conditions for the local stonemasons and specialist repairs team) an extensive fully-sheeted access scaffold with roof was erected. Yet, the first task was to retrieve the various stones; no easy task considering the size and weights involved. To accommodate these loads the scaffold had to be adapted to include a high-performance lifting jib to safely set the stones down in the graveyard below. The stones were taken to the workshop of West Country masons, laid out and carefully examined in order to 'dry build' the pinnacle out of position, a challenge that was met within 48 hours. This exercise was vital to inform the complex schedule of repairs.

The approved works that ensued followed a tight and precise programme, a consequence, in part, of the heavy cost of the scaffold hire. The repair of the tower roof timberwork was a fairly straight forward task however the north aisle roof was more complex because of the serious damage caused to the trusses, gable end and wall by falling masonry. During the repair programme careful consideration was given to the historic fabric. Being able to identify periods of the building's development informed our 'repair as found' philosophy and therefore guided the conservation techniques and technologies deployed. Wherever possible, regardless of being a visible or invisible

Fig. 6
Early work on St Kayna's at St Keyne. The pinnacle was completed blown clear of the tower. Author.

Fig. 7
Detail of missing pinnacle at St Kayna from the tower. Author.

repair, the medieval timberwork was retained and, where necessary, new oak was scarfed and pegged into the old timber. In addition, carpenters skilfully replicated the lost northern components of the trusses and rebuilt it entirely. In conjunction with the carpentry work, the stonemasons methodically scheduled and recorded the historic fabric before they took down the granite stone walls that had obviously taken direct impact from falling stones. The walls and tracery were expertly rebuilt and pointed with a lime sand mix before the glass that had been removed from the windows as a precaution was reinserted.

In the new edition of *Cornwall* the ceiling of the church is described as 'late C15 wagon roofs in N aisle and S transept, the transept roof with the wall-plate set on a granite moulded cornice'.[6] This Tudor work in the nave and chancel roofs was, in part, refurbished and restored in 1878 by Henry Elliot, a little known but relatively busy church restorer working in the county. Where parts of this historic structure had been lost, oak laths were laid to reform the barrel shape, and a traditional horse hair plaster mix using lime and sand was applied intermittently over many weeks due to the lengthy time lime takes to set. Where plaster roof bosses fell they were recovered and formed into new moulds using lime plaster before being fixed back at the truss joints

(Fig.4). Outside of the church the same care was exercised by the stonemasons who repaired the old stones and carved new and set about lifting them back up to the tower roof to reset them into position. The decision was taken to incorporate stainless steel pins between the courses to secure the stone in the pinnacle core. This omitted the need to incorporate the old dog cramps which was thought to have been the cause of the strike in the first place. Once done, the final job was to re-point in a lime sand mix.

The same conservation philosophies were applied to the damaged north-east pinnacle which was completely deconstructed and subsequently rebuilt in its original position with pinning between each course (Fig.5). Additional lightning protection for the tower was funded by the Parochial Church Council and consisted of a ring main conduction tape running around the inside face of the tower roof parapet with down tape and strike rods fitted to the top of each of the four pinnacles. The parapet tape was then earthed via two further down tapes to the north and south faces of the tower. In the event of a lightning strike these will discharge into earthing mats which are sited in the graveyard below, which should ensure the future safety of the building.

The church at St Keyne differs from Pillaton in that it was built from mudstone, a fine-grained sedimentary rock, which is decaying badly from severe weather exposure. As at Pillaton, Pevsner was rather dismissive of the church, he wrote 'A church of little interest architecturally or in its furnishings'.[7] Predictably Beacham is less indifferent than his forebear but does deflect to a simple technical description of the church 'C15 unbuttressed W tower of three stages with embattled parapet and crocketed pinnacles. The body of the church – nave, N aisle, S transept and S porch –was extensively rebuilt, especially on the S side, in restorations of 1868 and 1874–8 by J.P. St Aubyn'.[8]

In 2003 concerns were raised about the fragile condition of the tower which in turn prompted an English Heritage funded-project led by the team at LePage Architects. After discovering that the top section was shifting, it was arranged to core drill the structural ties along the full length of the tower and lay along each tower face just below the parapet crenelations. Although it was a concern that the pinnacles may fail due to their delicacy (caused by using weak materials) vertical ties were core drilled into each, so that an intersection of modern steel occurred at each corner of the tower. It was this intersection below the northeast pinnacle that attracted the lightning, the consequence of which was an explosion causing the pinnacle to fall apart (Figs.6 and 7). As at Pillaton the large granite top stone and finial fell into to the central valley coming to a halt after bouncing off and crushing the Victorian timbers in the north roof aisle. Due to the friability of the stone, little was left of the pinnacle. Fortunately, the 18th century slate memorials and the good quality 20th century stained glass survived undamaged.

Again working with the Ecclesiastical Insurance Company and English Heritage it was decided that the same team that dealt with St Odulph's should be deployed. Complex scaffolding was erected around the tower to facilitate lifting the stone safely out of the valley of the roof. From there it was gently placed on ground level whilst the masons undertook a detailed schedule of stone locations around the parapet corner where the pinnacle had been lost. This was a long process of numbering and recording each separate stone and its place in the tower wall. After discussion with the structural engineer and masons it was decided not to replace the steel ties, as the design and use of

Fig. 8
Completed repairs at St Kayna. Author.

them requires core drilling into established stonework which then has to be pumped with grout, which seeps through binding deep within the wall.

The priority of our work schedule was to create a strong, bound, masonry structure ensuring minimum scaffold hire time. Given that the tower wall structure was lost, the tie would not function correctly and an easier and quicker method would be to lay specialist, smaller helical steel ties in larger numbers across the courses of the parapet wall as it was built up. This strategy was adopted on both the lost and shaken pinnacle stones at each course, with an additional thicker vertical tie up through their centres. Moreover, as these high-level masonry repairs progressed, attention was given to the Victorian roof timbers that were damaged by the dislodged masonry. Conscious that the roof comprised of scissor trusses and arch bracing we retained our philosophy of restoring the fabric in sympathy with the old and thus enabled the new and old to be skilfully, methodically and traditionally-jointed together. Local slaters finished the work with second hand Cornish slates while internally, the ceiling was plastered and decorated using the same methodologies as at Pillaton. Once again the tower had its lightning protection upgraded to include a ring beam of conducting tape along the inside face of the parapet, with a strike rod fitted to each pinnacle, all earthing to ground with two down tapes positioned on the north and south sides of the tower (Fig.8).

The aims of restoration were threefold. First, to repair the damage caused to both towers to withstand attack by weather in all its forms. Second, careful consideration had to be given to the reinstatement of the historic church detail without being stringently and solely constrained to conservation principles. Hence, some balance was adopted between the philosophy of 'repair as found' as championed by the Society for the Protection of Ancient Buildings (SPAB) and the practicalities of deploying modern interventions and technologies. Third, the programme of works was delivered with a full understanding of the history of the building and with full and open dialogue with interested parties. It is this holistic approach that has allowed the retention of both churches architectural integrity while giving the repairs some longevity against the prevailing weather.

Notes
1. Pevsner (1951), p.125.
2. Pevsner (2014), p.443.
3. *Western Morning News*, 23 January 2013.
4. *Cornish Times*, 10 January 2014.
5. These are dated 1742, 1746 and 1772.
6. Pevsner (2014), *Ibid*.
7. Pevsner (1951), p.168.
8. Pevsner (2014), p.573.

Biographies of contributors

Paul Holden, FSA, is House and Collections Manager for the National Trust at Lanhydrock House in Cornwall and Chairman of the Cornish Buildings Group. He has published widely on architecture, history and curatorial issues, his most recent publications include *The Lanhydrock Atlas* (Cornwall, 2010); '"Of Things Old and New": The Work of Richard Coad and James M. MacLaren', in Jason Edwards and Imogen Hart (eds.) in *The Aesthetic Interior* (Stroud, 2010); *The London Letters of Samuel Molyneux 1712–13* (London, 2011); 'Country House Technology at Lanhydrock House in Cornwall' in Paul Barnwell and Marilyn Palmer (eds.), *Country House Technology* (Stamford, 2012); 'A Cornish Parish Torn Apart' in Terence Dooley and Christopher Ridgeway (eds.) *The Country House and the Great War* (Dublin, 2016) and 'William Wynford (fl.1360–1404), Retained Master Mason to William of Wykeham' in *Winchester: Archaeology and Memory* (forthcoming). Paul is currently writing *Country Houses of Cornwall*. He is a regular reviewer for, amongst others, the Society of Antiquaries of London, Society of Architectural Historians of Great Britain and the Royal Society.

John Allan, FSA, is past President of the Devon Archaeological Society, President of the Friends of Devon Archives, Consultant Archaeologist to the Dean and Chapter of Exeter Cathedral and Archaeological Adviser to Glastonbury Abbey. He has served as Joint Editor of the Society for the international journal Post-Medieval Archaeology, Member of Council of the Society for Medieval Archaeology, Member of Council of the Society of Cathedral Archaeologists, a Trustee of the Devon Historic Buildings Trust, Editor of the Devon Archaeological Society between 1984 and 1997 and Curator of Antiquities at Exeter Museum between 1984 and 2004. John has published widely on different aspects of medieval and later archaeology of south-west England, including ceramics, church architecture, monastic sites, castle architecture, medieval houses, and Anglo-Saxon towns and coins.

Peter Beacham, OBE, FSA, PhD, has written extensively about the buildings of the south-west. He was for many years Conservation Officer at Devon County Council and retired in 2011 as Director of Heritage Protection at English Heritage. He is currently a member of the Architectural Panel of the National Trust. Over the course of a decade Peter revised and expanded Nikolaus Pevsner's *The Buildings of England: Cornwall* (Yale University Press, 2014) and is now editing a volume on the architectural history of Buckfast Abbey to celebrate the Abbey's millennium in 2018.

Simon Crosbie, MA in Archaeological Conservation and a director at Le Page Architects where he specialises in historic buildings and conservation practice. In 1988 Simon worked extensively on Plymouth's historic Barbican and more recently took a key role in the decade-long conservation and refurbishment of Sir John Rennie's Royal William Yard in Plymouth, Devon.

Andrew Langdon is from Wadebridge. He is an authority on Cornwall's medieval stone crosses, an expertise that was acknowledged by the Cornwall Heritage Trust when he was presented with their annual Heritage Champion award. His publication *Wade-Bridge: Notes on the History of the Fifteenth Century Bridge* (The Federation of Old Cornwall Societies, 2012) won the 2012 Holyer an Gof Award.

Joanna Mattingly, FSA, PhD, came down to Cornwall to teach local history and Cornish church architecture in 1985, before switching to museum work. It took at least ten years before she had anything new to say about Cornish church building and is still learning. She is currently a freelance lecturer, museum consultant and serves on the Council of the Cornish Buildings Group.

Patrick Newberry, FRSA, researches the history of individual British country houses, lecturing regularly on Leith Hill Place, Ralph Vaughan Williams's childhood home, for the National Trust. He has been exploring the historical buildings of Cornwall from an early age and, fifty years on, still enjoys the thrill of new discoveries. He has supplemented his academic interest in historical architecture with practical experience of caring for old buildings, overseeing the restoration and maintenance of a near derelict rectory in East Cornwall. Patrick is a Council member and Awards Administrator for the Cornish Buildings Group

Charles O' Brien is series Editor of the Pevsner Architectural Guides and author or co-author and contributor to several of the revised volumes including *Bedfordshire, Huntingdonshire and Peterborough*; *London 5: East*, *Yorkshire West Riding: Leeds, Bradford and the North*; *Hampshire: Winchester and the North*; and *Sussex: East* (Yale University Press).

Jeremy Pearson, AMA, was for some years Historic Properties Representative (later Curator) for the National Trust in Devon and Cornwall and has served on many local museum and heritage committees.

Ann Preston-Jones is an archaeologist working for both English Heritage and Cornwall Council. She has recently co-authored with Elisabeth Okasha a study of pre-Norman stone sculpture in Cornwall entitled *Corpus of Anglo-Saxon Stone Sculpture, XI, Early Cornish Sculpture* (University of Durham/ Oxford University Press/British Academy, 2014). This award winning book, part of a major series published by the British Academy, surveys the county of Cornwall and provides an analytical catalogue of its early sculpture, highlighting the particular distinctiveness of Cornish sculpture compared to other regions.

Rosamund Reid completed her MA in Victorian Studies at Royal Holloway College, University of London, in 1993 and her MPhil thesis on the life and work of George Wightwick was supervised by Professor Joe Mordaunt Crook.

Michael Swift is the stained glass adviser for the Diocese of Truro and for Truro Cathedral. He is the author of a forthcoming book on Truro Cathedral and numerous articles on Cornish glass. He has contributed to four volumes of Nikolaus Pevsner's *Buildings of England* series including the current *Cornwall* edition.

Michael Warner was brought up in St Ives. He has been an Anglican parish priest for 44 years and has served 40 years in the Diocese of Truro. He has an expertise on Cornish Anglican church buildings, and has served as a member, Secretary, and currently an advisor to the Truro Diocesan Advisory Committee for the Care of Churches. During this time he has compiled *A Gazetteer of works on Cornish Anglican Churches. 1700–2000*, as yet unpublished. Canon Warner was awarded with a Master of Philosophy degree from the University of Exeter (2006) for his dissertation 'To have and to hold? The parochial maintenance and enhancement of Cornish Anglican church buildings in the Twentieth-Century, and considerations for their future use'.

Alex Woodcock, FSA, PhD, is a former stonemason who spent six years conserving the iconic west front of Exeter cathedral. With a background in archaeology he completed a PhD on Romanesque and Gothic stonecarving in England and has since published on medieval architectural sculpture. Alex is currently researching material for a book on Romanesque stone-carving in Devon and Cornwall.

Index

Note: Page numbers in *italic* refer to figures.

Acland family 115–16
Acton Castle 89, 96
Adam, Robert 94
Adams brothers 98
Adams, M.B. 130
Agar Robartes family 123
Allom, Thomas *96*
Alne, Yorkshire 43
Antony House 87–8, *88*, *121*, *123*, *125*
Arlington, Devon 57, *61*
Ascot Priory: Society of the Most Holy Trinity 109
Aston, Mick 32

Bake House 88
Baldhu: St Michael's and All Angels 26
Baring-Gould, Sabine 114
Bartholomew de Castro 58
Basset, John Pendarves 89
Bath stone 127
Baxter, Ron 46
Beacham, Peter 103–4(nn2, 8); *see also* *Cornwall* (2014)
beakhead ornament *42*, *44*, *45*, 46
Beaupel family 57
Beaverbrook, Lord 128
Beer stone *50*, 51, 52, 55, 56, 57, 58, *59*, 60
Benson, Bishop Edward White 14, 103, 104, 109, 110, 127
Bere Ferrers, Devon 51, 58
Berkeley Castle 52, *54*

Betjeman, John 11, 13, 28, 29, 83, 91, 130; *Shell Guides* 15, 18, 20, 28–9, 83
Bettesworth-Trevanion, John 90–1, 97–8
Bickford-Smith, William 115
Bideford Bridge 66, 71
Bishop's Palace, Exeter 52
Bishop's Palace, St Columb 100
Bland, John 89
Blight, J.T. 31
Bloxham, Revd John Rouse 102n18
Board of Trade 71
Boconnoc House 89, 95
Bodmin: clock tower 117; County Lunatic Asylum 113–14; Priory 49, 60; St Petroc's church 13, 74, 77, 78
Bodrugan, Henry 76
Book of Kells 34
Borlase William *66*, 67
Boscawen, Admiral 124
Boswell, James 89
Boyce, G.A. 129n11
Brett, R.L. 115n12
Brettingham, Matthew 88
brick 86, 87
Bridgend church 136
Bristol: Cathedral 49, 51, *52*, *54*; St Mary Redcliffe *52*, *54*
Bronescombe, Bishop of Exeter 51
Brown, Capability 94, 101
Brown, H.M. 103(nn4, 7), 130
Bubb, James 127

Buckland Brewer 44, 45
Bucknall Estcourt, Lady 126
Bude: St Michael and All Angels church 116
Building News 127
Buildings of England 18–22, 24, 25, 28
Buller family 122
Burges, William 14, 123–4, 125, 128
Butterfield, William 99, 102n18, 118, 131

Caerhayes Castle 90–1, *97*, 97–8, 99
Calendar of Patent Rolls 66
Callington: St Mary's church 74, 75, 132, 135
Calstock church 75, 81, 136
Calverleigh Court 129n11
Camborne church 79
Camden Society 116, 118
Campbell, Colen 87, 89
Campbell, John 15
Carclew House 89, 96
Cardinham: Cornish cross *34*
Carew family 88
Carminow, John 77
Carpenter, Richard Cromwell 99
Carpenter, William 77
Castle Hill, Devon 95
castles 46, 98; Acton 89, 96; Berkeley 52, *54*; Caerhayes 90–1, *97*, 97–8, 99; Eastnor, Herefordshire 123, 125; Ince 86; Luscombe, Devon 98; Pentillie 83, 94, 98, 99, 140; Sudeley, Gloucestershire 123; Tregenna 89, 96
Castletown, Dublin 88
Catchfrench 89, 97, 100
cathedrals: Bristol 49, 51, 52, *54*; Exeter 13, 49, *50*, 51, 52, 53, 55, 57, 58, *59*, 60, *61*, 62; Plymouth 125; Truro 14, 28, 100, 103, 104–5, 107, 110, 127–8; Wells 49, 52

Chapel Point, Mevagissey 15
Charles II 84
Chasewater church 99
Cherry, Bridget 21, 22n1, 58
Chichester, Francis J. 125
Chichester Nagle, Joseph 125, 129n11
Chichester Nagle, Lady Henrietta 125
Christchurch (Dorset) 55, *56*, 57
Church Rate 131, 136n7
churches 94; All Saints, Killigrew Street, Falmouth *27*; All Saints, Margaret Street, London 118; Bodmin Priory 49, 60; Bridgend 135; Calstock 75, 81, 135; Camborne 79; Chasewater 99; Christchurch (Dorset) 55, *56*, 57; Constantine 75; Crediton *53*; Creed 133; Crowan 135; Cury 43, 76, 78; Decorated style 49, 52, 55, 57, *59*, 60; Devon 49, 52, 57; Duloe 13, 76, 77–8, 135; Fowey 13, 60, 76, 80; Godolphin in Breage 81; Greyfriars, Exeter 52; Gunnislake 135; Gunwalloe 81; Gwennap 134, 135; Gwinear 75, *75*, 76; Hessenford 135; Kea 98; King Charles the Martyr, Falmouth 81, 94; Lanlivery 13, 75, 76, *78*; Lanteglos-by-Camelford 131; Launceston Priory 12–13, 49, 52–5, *53*, *54*, *56*, 60, 62; lightning strikes 15, 137–9, 143, 144–5; Lostwithiel 60; Mabe 131; Marazion 135; Mawgan in Pydar 76; Mawnan 131; medieval churches 49; Mevagissey 131; Mylor 81; new Victorian churches 131–2, 135; North Petherwin 79; Ottery St Mary 49, 50, 51, 52, *53*, 55, *56*, 57, 58; Paul 74; Penponds 135; Perpendicular architecture 13, 74–81, 94; Perranarworthal 134; Perranuthnoe 135; porches *80*, 80–1; Probus 78; Redruth 99; restoration and enhancement 27, 28, 130–3, 137–45; Rialton, St Columb Minor

81; Sennen 74; Sherborne Abbey 49, 50, 51; Sheviock 13, 55, *59*; South Hill 55, 58, *59*, *60*; St Alban's Holborn 109; St Andrew's, Plymouth 77; St Anthony-in-Roseland 43; St Austell 13, 75, 76–7, 81; St Buryan 30n8; St Carantoc, Crantock 14, 74, 103–10, *105*, *106*, *107*, *108*, *109*; St Cleer 74; St Columb Major 74; St Cuby, Tregony 132–3; St Day 99; St Enodoc 29, 131; St Germans *10*, 13, 43, 55, 57, 58, *59*, *60*, 75; St Gluvias, Penryn 96; St Hilary 99; St Issey 135; St Ive 13, 55, 57, 58, *59*, *60*, 61; St Ives 74, 75, 76, 78; St James, Kilkhampton 43, 44, 46, 123; St James, Shebbear 44, 45, *46*; St John the Baptist, Penzance 99, *131*, 135; St John's, Devoran 99; St John's-in-the-fields, Halsetown 135; St John's (RC), Tiverton 129n11; St John's, Treslothan 115, *116*, 135; St Just-in-Penwith 74, 75–6, 134; St Kayna's, St Keyne 15, 138, *138*, *141*, *142*, 143–5, *144*; St Martin by Looe 74; St Martin's, Liskeard 74, 77, 78; St Mary Magdalene, Launceston 75, 78; St Mary Redcliffe, Bristol 52, 54; St Mary the Virgin, Par 26, 99, 100, *100*; St Mary's, Callington 74, 75, 132, 135; St Mary's, Truro 78, 96, 127, 136n7; St Michael and All Angels, Baldhu 26; St Michael and All Angels, Bude 116; St Michael Penkevil 13, 57–8, *59*, 62; St Michael's, Helston 96; St Michael's, Newquay 100; St Morwenna, Morwenstow 12, 41, 41–2, *42*, 43–4, *44*, 45, *45*, 46–7, 81; St Neot 57, 58; St Odulph's, Pillaton 15, 137, *137*, 138–43, *139*, *140*, 145; St Peter's, Flushing 116–17, *117*; St Petroc's, Bodmin 13, 74, 77, 78; St Petroc's, Padstow 13, *37*, 75, 76, *76*, 77; St Philip and St James, Maryfield, Antony 26, *27*, 99, 104; St Sidinus, Sithney 76, 80; St Stedyana's, Stithians *132*, 133–4, 135; St Stephen's, Launceston 43, 74; St Teath 81; St Torney, North Hill 78, *79*; St Uda's, St Tudy *133*, 135; St Veep 77; St Winnow 13, 77; St Wyllow, Lanteglos-by-Fowey *25*, 25–6, 131; Stratton 74; 'three-hall' form 25–6, 74, 79; Treleigh 135; Trythall 135; Tuckingmill 135; Tywardreath 55, *59*; Werrington church 94, *95*; *see also* cathedrals; Glasney College, Penryn

Churchill, Winston 128

Clarendon House, Piccadilly 87

Clark, Kenneth 14

Clayton and Bell 104, 110, 128

Clifton-Taylor, Alec 21

Clowance 89, 135

Coad, Richard 14, 123, 128n2, 131

Cocks, Agneta (née Pole Carew) 121, 122

Cocks Biddulph bank 122, 128n2

Cocks, Charles Lygon 14, *121*, 121–8; early life 121, 122; army career 122–3; design 124–5, 126–7; marriage and family 125–6, 129n10; photography 121, 126; Treverbyn Vean 121, *122*, *123*, 123–6, *124*, *126*, 128; Truro Cathedral 127–8; death and obituary 128

Cocks, Charlotte 126

Cocks family 121, 122, 125

Cocks, Josephine (née Chichester Nagle) 125, 128

Cocks, Octavius 125

Cocks, Thomas 121–2

Cocks, William 122

Coleridge, Derwent 114, 115

Coleridge, Samuel Taylor 114

Collier, W.F. 112n2
Collins, Captain 117
Colshull, Sir John 78
Colvin, Howard 14, 94, 112
Combe Flory, Somerset 57
Comper, Sebastian 100
Comper, Sir Ninian 100
Constantine church 75
Coom, Henry 67
Cornelius, Alfred 100
Cornish Anglicisation 94
Cornish Heritage Trust 22
Cornish Times 128, 138n4
Cornwall (1951) 11, 13, 18, 18–19, 22, 28, 29, 30, 31, 65, 81, 83, 91, 137, 143
Cornwall (1970) 20–1
Cornwall (2014) 11–12, 14, 15, *20*, *22*, 23–30, 31, 55, 74, 76, 78, 86, 114–15, 123, 130–1, 137, 142, 143
Cornwall Archaeological Unit 12–13, 51, 52
Cornwall County Council 72
Coryton family 99
Cotehele 26, 84, 96
country houses 13–14, 83–91, 100, 102n19; Antony 87–8, *88*, 121, 123, 125; Bake 88; Boconnoc 90, 95; Carclew 89, 96; Catchfrench 90, 97, 100; Clowance 90, 135; Cotehele 26, 84, 97; Croan 87; E-shaped houses 84, 85, 90; Godolphin 26, 86, *87*; Kelham Hall, Nottinghamshire 123; Lanhydrock 14, 26, 85–6, *86*, 90, 93, 123; Lewarne 100; Longleat 84; Luxstowe, Liskeard 99, 117; Menabilly 26, 87; Moorswater Lodge *98*, 99; Mount Edgcumbe 83–4, *84*, 95, 96; Nanswhyden 89, 96; Painshill, Surrey 97; Pelyn 85; Pencarrow 67, 83, 88, 117, *118*; Penheale Manor 83, 85; Penquite 117; Penstowe House 100; Place, Fowey 99; Port Eliot 83, 90, 97, 99; Prideaux Place 85; Restormel 97; Saunders Hill 90, *90*; Stoketon 97; Stourhead, Wiltshire 97; Stowe 84, 87, 94; Tehidy 89, 96; Thames-banks, Great Marlow 122; Trebartha Hall 90; Trebursye 99; Tregarden 85; Tregenna House 100; Tregothnan 83, 98–9, 100; Tregrehan House 117, *119*; Trehane 87; Trelissick 91; Trelowarren 96; Trereife 87; Trerice 26, 84–5, *85*; Trevarno Manor 115, *115*; Treverbyn Vean 14, 100, 121, *122*, *123*, 123–6, *124*, *126*, 128; Trewan Hall 14, 85, 86, 93–4; Trewithen 26, 88–9; Walton Hall, Warwickshire 123; Wanstead 89; Winter Villa, Plymouth 123; Wollaton Hall 84

County Sessions 69, 71
Courtenay, Edward 76
Courtenay, Hugh 76–7
Crace, J.C. 123, 125
Crantock: St Carantoc church 14, 74, 103–10, *105*; architectural layout 105, 110; life of St Carantoc *107*, *108*, 108–9; Marian iconography *106*, 107–8; restoration 103–4, 110; roof bosses 107; stained glass windows 104, 105–10, *106*, *107*, *108*, *109*
Crediton church *53*
Creed church 133
Croad, Abel 88
Croan 87
Crook, Mordaunt 100
Croome Court, Worcestershire 94
cross bases 36, *37*; Doniert Stone 32, 36, *37*; Gulval 12, 31–5, *32*, *33*, 36, 38, *37*; Ireland 36, 37; Lanhadron, St Ewe *37*; Margam, Wales 36; Padstow churchyard *37*
crosses *32*, *34*, 37–8, 39

Crowan church 135
Cury church 43, 76, 78
Dalmeny, Edinburgh 99
Damant, William 113
Daniell, Thomas 91
Darlyon, Colonel Edward 117
De l'Orme, Philibert 86
Decorated Gothic 12, 100
Decorated ('Middle Pointed') style 49, 52, 55, 57, *59*, 60
Dehio, George 11, 18
Devon: churches 49, 52, 57; Romanesque sculpture 43, 44, 45, 47
Devoran: St John's church 99
Dodds, Pam 76
Domesday Book 39
Doniert Stone 32, 36, *37*
Donnington Hall, Leicestershire 98
Doric style 91
Duchy Nursery, Lostwithiel 100–1, *101*
Duloe church 13, 76, 77–8, 135
Durham: cross-head 36
Dysert O'Dea, Co. Clare 39

Early English architecture 100
Early Gothic 42
early medieval sculpture 32
Eastlake, Charles 14
Eastnor Castle, Herefordshire 123, 125
ecclesiastical architecture 12–13; *see also* Gothic architecture; Gothic Revival
Ecclesiastical Insurance Company 140, 143
Ecclesiologists 99, 100, 116
Edgcumbe, Caroline, Countess of Mount Edgcumbe 122
Edgcumbe, Ernest, 3rd Earl of Mount Edgcumbe 123, 127
Edgcumbe family 81, 84, 95, 122
Edgcumbe, Richard, 2nd Baron 95
Edgcumbe, William, 4th Earl of Mount Edgcumbe 127
Edwards, Thomas 88, 95
Egloshayle 65, 66, 71; Bridge House 68; King's chapel 66
Eliot family 97
Elliot, Henry 142
elvan stone 78, 84, 128
engine houses *24*, 24–5
English Heritage 22, 140, 143
Evangelists *35*, *36*, 38; Callington 75; Gulval cross base 12, 33–5; stone sculpture 36; symbolism 33–5
Eveleigh, John 89
Exeter Cathedral 13, 49, *50*, *53*, 55, 58, *59*, 60, *61*; tomb of Bishop Stapledon 57, *60*; workshop 51, 52, 57, 62
Exeter Diocesan Architectural Association 133
Exeter Diocese 26
Exeter: Greyfriars church 52

Falmouth: All Saints church *27*; King Charles the Martyr church 81, 94; Royal Cornwall Philosophical Society 115
Falmouth, Edward Boscawen, 4th Viscount 98–9
Ferrers, William 58
Ferrey, Benjamin 99
Fiennes, Celia 87
Flushing: St Peter's church 116–17, *117*
fonts 43, 45
Foulston, John 14, 113
Fowey: church 13, 60, 76, 80; Place 99
Fox, Barclay 115
Fox, Robert Were 115

Galilei, Alessandro 88
Geldart, Revd Ernest 131

George, Prince Regent 97
Gibbs, James 88, 89
Gittos, Moira and Brian 62
Glanville, Lt George 126–7
Glasney College, Penryn 12–13, 49, *50*, 51, 52, *53*, 60
Glencross, William 99, 117
Glynne, Sir Stephen 131
Godolphin church 81
Godolphin House 26, 86, *87*
Godolphin, Sidney 87
Godolphin, Sir William 86
Goskar, Tom 32
Gothic architecture 14, 93, 101; Decorated Gothic 12, 100; ecclesiastical 32, 42, 81, 94; secular 14, 26–7, 83, 85, 86, 89, 90, 93–4; Gothic Revival 14, 26; Arts and Crafts Gothic 27; ecclesiastical 26–8, *27*, 94, *95*, 96, 98, 99–100, 103–4; Ecclesiologists Gothic 99, 100; Perpendicular Gothic 81, 94; Picturesque Gothick 89, 90, 96, *97*, 97, 99, 100–1, *101*; Rococo Gothick 89, 94, 95, 96; secular 89, 94–9, *95*, *96*, 100–1, *101*, 102n19, 121; Tudor Gothic 83, 85, 89, 95, 97, 99, 116, 117, 121; *see also* Crantock: St Carantoc church
Grandisson, Bishop of Exeter 51, 58
Grandisson, Otto and Beatrice 57, 58
granite 83; domestic use 85, 86, 89; ecclesiastical use 12, 31, 33, 36, 37, 49, 77, 78, 79, 81; quarries 79, 127; Truro Cathedral 127–8; Wade-Bridge 71
Gregor, Sarah 90–1
Grylls, Humphrey: Monument, Helston 99, *114*, 114–15
Gulval church: cross 37–8, *38*; cross base 12, 31–5, *32*, *33*, 36; restoration 133; St Mark 34, *35*
Gunnislake church 136

Gunwalloe church 81
Gwatkin, R.L. 98
Gwennap: church 134, 136; population 134
Gwinear church 75, *75*, 76

Hall, Teresa 32
Halliday, F.E. 65n1
Hallworthy-Mitchell turnpike 68
Halsetown: St John's-in-the-fields church 136
Halton, Lancashire: cross-shaft 36
Hamble, Arthur 127
Hamilton, Charles 97
Hansom, J.A. and C.F. 125
Harkness Gospels *see* Landévennec Gospels
Harries, Susie 25, 29
Harrison, Henry 83, 97
Hartland Abbey 45, 47
Hartwell, Clare *21*
Haslam, Revd William 131
Hawker, Revd R.S. 12
Hawkins, Phillip 88, 89
Hawkins, Thomas 89
Hawksmoor, Nicholas 94, 96
Hayward, John 51, 136n13
Helland Bridge 69
Helston: Grammar School 99, 114; Humphrey Grylls memorial 99, *114*, 114–15; St Michael's church 96
Henderson, Charles 13, 58, 71
Henderson, James 71
Henry I 45–6
Henry II 46, 47
Henry VI 76
heraldic tiles 52
Herbert, Catherine 94–5
Heritage Lottery Fund 22
Hessenford church 136

Hicks, James 28
Hicks, William 114
Hill, Frederick Lobb 114
Hine and Odgers 132, 136n13
Hine, James 131
Hingeston-Randolph, Revd Francis 131
Hingston Down 79
Hoare, Henry 97
Holland, Henry 91
Holton, John 78
Hoskins, W.G. 23
Hussey, Christopher E.C. 95
Hutchens, Charles 99, 132

Ince Castle 86
Irish cross bases 36–7
Irish high crosses 39

Jeffery, Paul 104n9
Jenkin, Silvanus William 71
Jenkins, Simon 41–2
John de Ferrers 58
John Hardman and Co, Birmingham 125
Johnson, John 97
Joy, William 13, 49, 51, 52, 62

Kayle, Phillipa (née Trenoweth) 77
Kayle, William 77
Kea church 98
Kelham Hall, Nottinghamshire 123
Kent, William 14
Kidd, Janet 128
Kilkhampton: manor 46; rectory 123; St James church 43, 44, 46, 123
Kilpeck, Herefordshire 43
Kylwyth, Laurence 76

Lacy, Edmund, Bishop of Exeter 75

Ladock font 43
Lake, William 89, 96, 124–5
Landévennec Gospels 34, 35, 38
Landkey, Devon 57, *61*
Lane, Allen 17
Langley, Batty 89, 96
Lanhadron, St Ewe: cross base *37*
Lanherne: Penwith group cross *34*, 35
Lanhydrock House 14, 26, 85–6, *86*, 90, 123; Gatehouse 86, *86*, 93
Lanisley 31, 38
Lanivet: Cornish cross *34*, 36
Lanlivery church 13, 75, 76, *78*
Lanreath font 43
Lanteglos-by-Camelford: church 131; rectory 102n18
Lanteglos-by-Fowey: St Wyllow's church *25*, 25–6, 131
Lantewy stone 128
Lantyan manor 76
Lapidge, Edward 113
Latham, Captain Frank 28, *29*
Launceston: Priory 12–13, 49, 52–5, *53*, *54*, *56*, 60, 62; St Mary Magdalene church 75, 78; St Stephen's church 43, 74; Town Hall 100
Le Page Architects 15, 143
Leland, John 66
Lemon, William 89
Leofric, Bishop of Exeter 39
Leofric Gospels 34, *36*, 39
Leverhulme Trust 19
Lewarne house 100
lightning strikes 15, 137–9, 143, 144–5
limestone 84
Lindisfarne Gospels 34
Liscombe, R.W. 98
Liskeard
Luxstowe House 99, 117; St Martin's church 74, 77, 78

London: All Saints church, Margaret Street 118; London Bridge 66; Survey of London 18
Longleat, Wiltshire 84
Looe: St Martin by Looe 74
Lostwithiel church 60
Loveday, John 87
Lovibond, John 65, 66, 67
Luscombe Castle, Devon 98
Lutyens, Edwin 83
Lycett Green, Candida 11, 15, 29

Mabe church 131
Marazion church 135
Margam, Wales: cross base 36
Marriott's Shaft, South Wheal Frances, Carn Brea *24*
Marsden, Philip 28
Martyn, John 71
Maryfield, Antony: rectory 123; St Philip and St James church 26, *27*, 99, 104
Mattingly, Jo 58
Mawgan in Pydar church 76
Mawnan church 131
Menabilly 26, 87
Methodism 26
Mevagissey: Chapel Point 15; church 131
Millman, Bishop of Calcutta: tomb 126, *127*
Moira, Earl of 98
Molesworth St Aubyn family 88, 117
Montgomery, Field Marshall Bernard 128
Moorswater Lodge, Liskeard *98*, 99
Morice family 94–5
Morice, Sir William 94, 95
Morris, Richard 51, 52, 95
Morwenstow: St Morwenna church 12, 41, 41–2, *42*, 43–4, *44*, *45*, 45, 46–7, 81
Mount Edgcumbe 83–4, *84*, 95, *96*
Mowl, Tim 87
Moyle, John 88
mudstone 143
Mylne, Robert 90
Mylor church 81

Nanfan, Sir John 76, *76*
Nanswhyden House 89, 96
Nash, John 90–1, 97–8
Neale, J.P. 99
Nesfield, William Eden *119*
Newenham Abbey, Axminster 52
Newquay: St Michael's church 100
Newton Ferrers 94
Nicholas de Derneford 52
Non-Conformists 99, 134, 135
North Hill: St Torney church 78, *79*
North Petherwin church 79

O'Brien, Charles 28
Observer 20
Okasha, Elisabeth 12
oolite 128
Orme, Nicholas 51, 108n22
Ottery St Mary church 49, *50*, 51, 52, *53*, 55, *56*, 57, 58

Padstow: St Petroc's church 13, 37, 75, 76, *76*, 77
Painshill, Surrey 97
Palladian architecture 83, 86, 87, 89, 95, 96
Palladio, Andrea 87
Par: St Mary the Virgin 26, 99, *100*
Park Place, Henley on Thames 95
Parker, Richard 52
Parsons, Father George Metford 14,

103, *103*, 104, 105, 107, 108, 109–10
Pascoe, Joseph 89
Paul church 74
Paul Mellon Centre for Studies of British Art 21
Pearson, John Loughborough 14, 28, 99, 100, 104, 127, 131
Pelyn House 85
Pelynt: parsonage house and school 117
Pembroke, Henry Herbert, 9th Earl of 90, 95
Pencarrow House 67, 83, 88, 117, *118*
Pendarves, Edward William 115, 116
Pendarves family 115, 116
Pengelly Barton (*formerly* Treverbyn Vean) 128
Penguin Books 17, 18–19, 21; *An Outline of European Architecture* (1942) 17; *Leaves of Southwell* (1945) 17; *Pelican History of Art* 18
Penheale Manor 83, 85
Penlee Point 95
Penmayne, St Minver Lowlands 65
Penponds church 136
Penquite house 117
Penryn: St Gluvias church 96
Penstowe House, Kilkhampton 100
Pentewan stone 13, 76, 77, 128
Pentillie Castle 83, 94, 98, 99, 140
Penzance: Jubilee Pool 28, 29; Natural History and Antiquarian Society 122; St John the Baptist church 99, *131*, 135
Perpendicular church architecture 13, 74–81, 94; church widening 74–5; pier types 74, 75–6; towers 74, 75, 76, 78, 81
Perranarworthal church 134
Perranuthnoe church 136
Peter, Otho B. 28
Peverell, Hugh 47

Pevsner Architectural Guides 17–22; *Architectural Glossary* 22, *22*; *Buildings of England* 18–22, 24, 25, 28; *City Guides* 21, *22*; *Devon* (1954) 23; *Devon* (2014) 58; *Manchester* (2000) *21*; *South Devon* (1952) 58; *see also Cornwall* (1951); *Cornwall* (1970); *Cornwall* (2014)
Pevsner Books Trust 21
Pevsner, Lola 19–20
Pevsner, Nikolaus 11–12, 13, 15, *17*, 17–21, 24, 49; *see also* Penguin Books; Pevsner Architectural Guides
Philip, John Birnie 124
Phillpotts, Canon 127
Phillpotts, Henry, Bishop of Exeter 99
Pillaton: St Odulph's church 15, 137, *137*, 138–43, *139*, *140*, 145
Pinwell, Violet 28, 30n8
Piper, John 28
Pitt, Thomas 95
Pitzhanger Manor 90
Place, Fowey 99
plasterwork 84, 85, 86, 89
Plymouth: Athenaeum 113, 114; St Andrew's church 77; St Mary and St Boniface Cathedral 125; Winter Villa 123
Pole Carew family 121–3
Pole Carew, Reginald 121
Polperro 28
Polyphant stone 134
Popham, Christopher 115
Port Eliot 83, 89, 90, 97, 99
Porth-en-Alls *6*, 15
Portland stone 87
Pratt, Roger 87
Preston-Jones, Ann 12
Prideaux Place 85
Probus church 78
Prynne, George Fellowes 131, 132

Pugin, A.W.N. 99, 102n18, 123, 125
Pusey, Edward Bouverie 109
Pydar 65

Queen Anne style 87

Radcliffe, Enid 20, 21
Radnor House, Twickenham 95
Ramble, Roderick (pseudonym) *see* Wightwick, George
Rawlings, Thomas 90
Rawlinson, Charles 89–90, 97
Reading Abbey, Berkshire 46
Redruth church 99
Reeve, J.A. 136n13
Reformation 79–81
Renaissance architecture 84, 86, 87–9
Repton, Humphry 90, 97, 98
Restormel house 97
Rialton, St Columb Minor 81
RIBA *see* Royal Institute of British Architects
Rice, Henry 14, 28, 123
Richard I 47
Richards, William 90
Richowe, Richard 77
Robartes, John, 1st Earl of Radnor 93
Robartes, John, 4th Earl of Radnor 95
Robert, Count of Mortain 45
Robert, Earl of Gloucester 46
Robinson, Peter Frederick 91
Rock-Padstow ferry 68
Rodwell, Warwick 26
Roland, Archdeacon of Exeter 39
Romanesque sculpture 43; Devon 43, 44, 45, 47; patronage 47; St Anthony-in-Roseland 43; St German's church 43; St James church, Kilkhampton 43, 44, 46; St Morwenna, Morwenstow *41*, 41–2, *42*, 43–4, *44*, *45*, 46; St Stephen's, Launceston 43
Roscarrock House, St Endellion 26, *26*
Roseberry, Earl of 99
Rowse, A. L. 13, 72
Rowtor, Bodmin Moor 79
Royal Brighton Pavilion 90
Royal Commission 18
Royal Fine Art Commission 71
Royal Institute of British Architects (RIBA) 112, 113

Sam, John 77
Saunders Hill 90, *90*
Schilling, Dr R. 22n3
Schmoller, Hans 20
Scott, George Gilbert 14, 123, 124
Sedding, Edmund Harold 27–8, 30n8, 42, 47, 103, 110, 131–2, 136n13
Sedding, John Dando 27, 27–8, 109, 131–2
Sennen church 74
Serlio, Sebastiano 84, 85
Shebbear 47; St James church 44, 45, *46*
Shell Guides 18, 20, 28–9, 83
Sheppard, George *85*
Sherborne Abbey 49, *50*, 51
Sheviock church 13, 55, *59*
Shute, John 85
Simpson, Derek 20–1
Sithney: St Sidinus church 76, *80*
slate 78, 132, 143, 144
Sleman, Harry 78
Smythson, Robert 84
Soane, Sir John 90, 97, 113
Society for the Protection of Ancient Buildings (SPAB) 145
Somers, Earl 123, 125
Somers family 125
South Hill church 55, 58, *59*, *60*
spirit of place 11, 28–30

St Alban's Holborn 109
St Aubyn, Catherine (née Morice) 94
St Aubyn, James Piers 14–15, 100, 130, 135n1; church restoration 130–5, 143; new churches 132, 135, 136n13
St Aubyn, Sir John 94, 95
St Austell church 13, 75, 76–7, 81
St Breock 65, 66
St Michael's chapel 66
St Buryan church 30n8
St Cleer church 74
St Columb Bank 27
St Columb Major: church 74; Old Rectory 26
St Day 28; church 99; clock tower 99
St Endellion: long cross 34
St Enodoc church 29, 131
St Faith's House of Mercy, Lostwithiel 100
St Germans church *10*, 13, 43, 55, 57, 58, *59*, *60*, 75
St Germans Priory 90
St Golvela 31
St Gwinear 75
St Hilary church 99
St Issey church 136
St Issey shrine 76, 77
St Ive church 13, 55, 57, 58, *59*, *60*, *61*
St Ives: church 74, 75, 76, 78; Knill Monument 96
St Ives Bridge, Cambridgeshire 66
St John *33*, 34, 35
St Just-in-Penwith: church 74, 75–6, 134; population 134
St Keyne: St Keyna's church 15, 138, *138*, *141*, *142*, 143–5, *144*
St Levan: cross 38
St Luke 33, 34, 35
St Mark *33*, 34, 35, *35*, *36*
St Matthew *33*, 34–5

St Mawgan rectory 102n18
St Michael Penkevil church 13, 57–8, *59*, 62
St Michael's Mount 26, 100; Blue Drawing Room 94, *95*
St Neot: church 57, 58; Cornish cross *34*
St Teath church 81
St Tudy: St Uda's church 133, 136
St Veep church 77
St Winnow church 13, 77
Stackhouse family 96
Stapledon, Bishop of Exeter 55, 57, *60*
Stephen, King 47
Stephens, Samuel 96
Stithians: St Stedyana's church *132*, 133–4, 135
Stockdale, F.W.L. 99
Stoketon house 97
Stourhead, Wiltshire 97
Stowe House 84, 86, 94
Stoyle, Mark 94
Stratton church 74
Strawberry Hill, London 95
Street, George Edmund 14, 26, 49, 55, 57, 60, 99, 100, 100, 131, 136n13
Suckling, Revd R.A. 109
Sudeley Castle, Gloucestershire 123

Talbot, France, Countess of Morley 118
Talbot, William Henry Fox 122
Tanner Trust 22
Taylor, George 113
Taylor, Sir Robert 88
Tehidy 89, 96
Tennyson, Alfred, Lord 118–19
Thames-banks, Great Marlow 122
Tilden, Philip *6*, 15
Tillie family 140
Tiverton: St John's (RC) church

129n11
tomb sculpture 55, 57, 58, *60*, 62, 126, 127
Trebartha Hall 90
Trebursye 99
Tregarden 85
Tregenna Castle 89, 96
Tregenna House, Michaelstowe 100
Tregony: St Cuby church 132–3
Tregothnan 83, 98–9, 100
Tregrehan, St Blazey 117, *119*
Trehane 87
Treleigh church 136
Trelissick 91
Trelowarren 96
Trenwith, Otto 76
Trereife 87
Trerice 26, 84–5, *85*
Tresham, Thomas 97
Treslothan 116; St John's church 115, *116*, 136
Trevail, Silvanus 28, 131, 136n13
Trevarno Manor, Sithney 115, *115*
Trevelver Farm, St Minver Highlands 67
Treverbyn Courtenay Manor 76
Treverbyn Vean 14, 100, 121, *122*, *123*, 123–6, *124*, *126*, 128
Trewan Hall 14, 85, 86, 93–4
Trewardale 117
Trewithen 26, 88–9
Trigg 65
Trinick, Michael 21
Truro: Cathedral 14, 28, 100, 103, 104–5, 107, 110, 127–8; St Mary's church 78, 96, 127, 136n7
Truro Kalendar 133
Trythall church 136
Tuckingmill church 136
Tute, Charles Edward 104, 110
Tyringham Hall 90
Tywardreath church 55, *59*

Vanbrugh, John 94
Victoria History of England 18
Victorian church restoration 27–8
Villiers, Hon. Frederick 125
Villiers, Lady Elizabeth 125
Vitruvius Britannicus 87, 88
Vulliamy, Lewis 100

Wade-Bridge 13, 65–72, *66*; Bridge House 68, 71; 'Bridge on Wool' 66; Bridge Trust 68, 69, 71; foundations 66–7, 72; plan *67*; quays 68, 71; traffic 68–9, 71, 72; widening of the bridge *68*, 68–72, *69*, *70*
Walpole, Horace 14, 95
Walton Hall, Warwickshire 123
Wanstead House 89
Ware, Isaac 89
Warwick, Earl of 76
Weale, John 117
Wells Cathedral 49, 52
Werrington church 94, *95*
West Briton 134
West Woolfardisworthy (Woolsery) 44, 45, 47
Western Daily Mercury 14, 119
Western Morning News 129n15, 137–8
White, Major General H.D. 126
White, William 14, 26, 27, 99, 100, 123, 131, 136n13
Wightwick, George 14, 99, 112–19, 132; early life 112–13; character 112, 113, 114, 118, 119; church architecture 115–17, *116*, 117; Low Church Liberalism 116, 117–18; secular architecture 113–15, *114*, 115, 117, *119*, 129n11; writing 112, 117–18, 119

Wilkins, William 83, 98, 99
Wilkins, William, Jnr 98, 99
William I 45
William of Worcester 65
Williamson, Elizabeth 21
Willimott, Revd William 131
Wills, Arthur 55
Witney, Thomas 49, 51, 62
Wollaton Hall, Nottinghamshire 84
Wood, John 89, 96
Wood, William 89, 96, *119*
Worsley, Dr Giles 101
Wren, Christopher 94, 96
Wyatt, James 98
Wyatville, Sir Jeffry 90, 99

Yale University Press 21
Yorke family 121, 123

zoo-anthropomorphic images 33, 34